MW00436651

"Marriage is about the gospel. The gospel is about marriage. Separating either from the other removes the essence of each. The entire Bible is about a bridegroom (Christ) caring for and consummating his love for his bride (the Church). Everett beautifully connects the story of Christ and the Church to marital help for you and your spouse. By sharing the ups and downs of his faith and the real raw truth of his own marriage, Everett offers profound relationship application for the reader through God's Word. His book is definitely a guide to lifelong love and marriage that lasts, but it also paints a vivid picture of Christ's deep love for his people, which is the most critical foundation any marriage can have."

—Hans Molegraaf
Marriage Revolution

"How does a former Marine personifying toxic masculinity and living with the shame of secret addictions become a committed follower of Christ, faithful husband, loving father, and minister of the gospel? Only by the grace of God. In *Husband & Wife*, Everett Tellez weaves his personal experience with Scripture to give an honest, compelling case for Christian marriage. He unabashedly writes of his spiritual and relational journey to challenge us all. Delving into the concepts of love, humility, and faith, he gives practical insight into living out the foundational principles necessary for marital success. You and your spouse will be blessed by this book!"

—Cliff and Jeani Poe
Founders and Directors
InfuseLife Ministries
Love Recon Seminars
Authors, *40 Days to a Thriving Relationship*

"Finally, a marriage book that deals truthfully about the mess we make of our relationships! My good friend Everett Tellez infuses each chapter with brutal honesty about his shortcomings as a husband and how God healed him through Jesus. Whether you are married or single, Christian or not, you need to hear the message of this book. It covers the sanctity of marriage but more importantly the inventor of marriage—God. Filled with redemption and romance, Everett shares the good news of God's love for all humankind."

—Reverend Peter Phillips
Pastor, Smithfield Baptist Church, Kentucky

HUSBAND & WIFE

A Guide to Lifelong Love and Marriage That Lasts

EVERETT TELLEZ

LUCIDBOOKS

Husband & Wife
A Guide to Lifelong Love and Marriage That Lasts

ISBN: 978-1-63296-582-0
eISBN: 978-1-63296-583-7

THIS BOOK IS DEDICATED TO

My wife, Brittany

I will never leave you or turn away from you.
Where you go I will go, and where you stay I will stay.

Table of Contents

Foreword   ix

Introduction   1

Chapter 1   Marriage Is about God   9

Chapter 2   Jesus Is Our Example   25

Chapter 3   The Holy Spirit Is Our Guide   43

Chapter 4   Stand against the Schemes   61

Chapter 5   Strengthen Your Faith for Marriage   77

Chapter 6   Happy Spouse, Happy House   93

Chapter 7   A Culture of Grace   109

Chapter 8   Humility Is Key   125

Chapter 9   All In   143

One Last Thing   159

Acknowledgments   163

Foreword

It wasn't how they planned it.

Benny Edwards was a life-giving presence who genuinely loved God and others. His faith was vividly displayed in how he served his family, church, and community. Benny was effortlessly generous, kind, courageous, confident, and humble. It didn't matter if he had the title of deacon in his church, a city councilman in his community, or no official title at all; he would always go above and beyond to help someone. Benny and my sister, Barbara, were high school sweethearts. She had a beautiful gift of Southern hospitality. As a gracious host, she would create warm and welcoming gatherings where people relaxed and connected around good food and conversation. Barbara had collected numerous sets of tableware with linens and decorations for all occasions but not for a business event; these supplies were for personal use in her church and community.

Barbara and Benny retired from careers in government agencies—his with the United States Postal Service and hers with the Social Security Administration, followed by a position with the Internal Revenue Service. Their retirement plans were simple—leverage their freedom to fully devote themselves to exercise their gifts of service and hospitality, side by side, loving God, loving each other, and loving others. Everything changed after one of those hospitality events when Barbara sensed something wasn't right. It all came on suddenly—nausea, difficulty seeing, knees buckling. Their world was spinning out of control. Benny held the love of his life in his arms, praying desperately and waiting for an ambulance to arrive. The paramedics arrived, and as her condition rapidly declined, they rerouted the ambulance to a hospital in Birmingham that was better equipped to handle what they believed was happening. And they were correct. The tests were clear. The hospital called in a specialist to remove a fist-sized tumor in her brain that had caused a stroke.

The golden years took a jolting detour. Hours of therapy and rehabilitation lay on the broken road ahead—learning how to walk . . . talk . . . bathe . . . dress . . . eat. All the take-for-granted functions that usually happen without thinking now demanded exhausting concentration to accomplish even the basics. Little by little, Barbara made progress and learned to communicate again. She adjusted to using her left hand in place of her right. She progressed from a walker to a cane to a reasonable level of unassisted mobility. But one thing would never improve. Removing a tumor that large from the human brain took with it her short-term memory. She would ask the same question multiple times in just 30 minutes—literally the exact same question . . . multiple times . . . in 30 minutes. No matter how slow and articulate the answers were, the information vanished from her memory in a few moments. If you paid close attention, you could almost see an answer settle at first with satisfaction in her eyes and then begin to fade as a curious and confused look emerged. Then the satisfaction would disappear entirely, followed by a repeat of the question, which started the cycle again. In the frequent spaces of these moments, I witnessed a most unusual and remarkable love. Each time Barbara asked the same question, Benny answered her with kindness, patience, and respect. He did this *every* time as if it were the first time.

Marriage is more than a document you file with the county. It's a covenant relationship. Covenant is not a common word in our culture, at least not on the street. As a matter of law, the words *covenant, contract,* and *agreement* seem to be interchangeable, but I think it's reduced to something we assume we can get out of with the right attorney. Dennis Rainey said this:

> *The Christian community has passively watched the dumbing down of the marriage covenant. Marriage has become little more than an upgraded social contract between two people—not a holy covenant between a man and a woman and their God for a lifetime.*[1]

In the Scriptures, covenant defines a solemn and binding relationship meant to last a lifetime. It is tied to the truth about the faithfulness of the covenant-keeping God. The word *covenant* is translated from the Hebrew word *berith,* which is derived from a root that means "to cut." In the days of the Old Testament when two people entered into a covenant, a goat or a lamb would be slain and its carcass cut in half. The two halves would be separated and placed on the ground. Then the two people who had formed the covenant would make their solemn promise by walking between the two halves saying, "May God do so to me [cut me in half] if I ever break this covenant with you and God." They didn't carve up animals in the wedding ceremony, but you get the feeling that a covenant in those days had a lot more substance than today.

When life doesn't turn out the way we planned, some people start looking for an exit. But my brother-in-law considered his marriage to my sister a covenant relationship that flowed from his covenant relationship with God. He modeled what the Bible means when it says in Ephesians 5:25 for husbands to "love your wives as Christ loved the church and gave himself up for it."

---

1. Dennis Rainey, "Ashley and Michael's Covenant," FamilyLife, 2013. https://www.familylife.com/articles/topics/marriage/getting-married/engagements-and-weddings/ashley-and-michaels-covenant.

Benny acknowledged in our conversations that it was the hardest thing he had ever done and sometimes seemed unbearable. But he confirmed that God would always give him the strength to carry on. He experienced the paradox truth of 2 Corinthians 12:10, "For when I am weak, then I am strong."

In 2020, the pandemic brought isolation from the social interactions that had kept Barbara's mind engaged and had given her the energy to keep moving physically. Her condition rapidly declined that year. Everything rapidly slowed down as she regressed both mentally and physically. Then in January 2021, Benny lost his final battle with cancer. Barbara was at first confused and afraid. She asked a couple of times when Benny was coming home, and we would try to explain. You could see her straining to process what had happened, and then the questions stopped. She finally acknowledged his passing and simply said, "Benny's not coming home, is he?"

It wasn't how they planned it.

But I think their story came to a graceful end. In Barbara's diminished mental and physical state, she seemed lost without Benny. In the days ahead, she quickly drifted away. After 58 years of marriage, the lives of these two soulmates ended about a month apart. Genuine faith is extraordinarily personal and powerful, especially when infused in a marriage. It displays itself with extreme generosity and self-sacrificial love. Husbands and wives become students of each other, and they understand throughout their marriage that school is always in session. Marriage becomes a perfect frame for God to display a beautiful portrait of His grace and truth through the good times, the difficult times, and the terrible times.

—Tierce Green
Co-Presenter of 33: The Series for Authentic Manhood
Director of Authentic Manhood Initiative and Good Feed Media
www.tiercegreen.com

Introduction

As far back as I can remember, I always wanted to be in a relationship. I can even recall my first crush. I was in pre-kindergarten at a Catholic School called Saint Elizabeth in South Texas. I don't ever remember talking to the girl; I just liked the way she looked. I liked everything about her—her hair, her eyes, and her smile. Butterflies fluttered around in my stomach every time I saw her. I can even tell you her name, but I won't. That probably wouldn't be the best way to start a marriage book. The point is that before I got married the first time (yep, the first time) I had been crushing on girls since nursery school. I didn't start dating, though, until fourth grade. Looking back, I recall how awesome some of those dating moments were, but today they are basically meaningless. All the silly love notes and holding hands, kissing and warm fuzzies, fantasizing and dreaming really serve no purpose in my life now, except to tell the story in this book.

Every year of grade school I had a different girlfriend, sometimes more than one. I know, I know—I don't sound like the typical protégé for marriage and relationships. It's because I'm not. If anything, I'm an expert on what not to do. But if God would let me go back in time, I imagine I'd do it all differently, not wanting to repeat the mistakes I made. I'd hope to apply the lessons I've learned for lots of reasons, but mainly because there's nothing I wouldn't give to have saved myself for my beautiful bride now. Her name is Brittany. My wifey-for-lifey is what I call her. I would gladly trade every relationship—all intimate highlights and satisfying moments from the past—to have her as my first and only love. Living with her every single day, I feel like I've robbed her of a piece of my heart and am making her live with the baggage of my past. It gets tough living in my hometown too. It's embarrassing bumping into an old flame, a summer fling, or a high school sweetheart. It's awkward telling my wife yet another tale of a failed relationship, a one-night stand from years and years ago, or a broken heart from back in the day. I've literally had to leave jobs and avoid certain places because of a few female skeletons in my closet.

It's ironic how the worst parts of my life led to the best part of my life. I'm still not sure why I had to go through fire to finally meet the woman of my dreams. I'm sure God knows; he's the one who brought Brittany to me. But I don't deserve her. My life as a divorced single guy was pretty bad. It was morally bad. I was no knight in shining armor; I was a thief in tattered rags. I didn't have the male profile that girls bring home to meet Mom and Dad. Instead, I had a rap sheet. I was the mug shot of a usual suspect with crimes so severe that sometimes I felt I didn't deserve to call myself a Christian. The Apostle Paul thought of himself as the worst of sinners (1 Tim. 1:15). I can relate. And if death is in the power of the tongue (Prov. 18:21), then my mouth has surely caused harm to others. I was once a bad parent, a terrible husband, and an even worse friend. I was once selfish in too many ways and schemed against many loved ones. I hardly qualify to have a wife or to be named among any church.

But that's the beauty and power of the gospel—the good news of Jesus Christ. His finished work on the cross has redeemed me. I no longer have to live in the haunting shadow of my past. In Christ, I can walk in the light. I never again have to fear the overcoming guilt of my dark history. I can look forward to the bright future of his unconditional love. By grace I have been saved through faith (Eph. 2:8). This is God's gift to me—undeserved grace out of his love and care for me. When Jesus saves, he makes a personal guarantee, one that remains in effect through God's commitment to his loved ones. And it stands the test of time magnificently through the power of the Holy Spirit. When I became a Christian, God promised to have me and hold me. He vowed to nurture me in sickness and in health, to protect me for richer or for poorer, and to love me for better or for worse. That unbreakable vow seals us together like a husband to a bride, like a compassionate foster parent to an orphan. The greatest gift and honor is having God for a father. As his child, everything I receive from him is a blessing, a gift. My wife is a gift. My kids are gifts. My job is a gift because it enables me to sustain my family's health and well-being. My church is a gift because it grows me and my family. It builds us up, encourages us, and spiritually feeds us. The power of salvation in Christ that creates newness of life is a gift. God's Word is also a gift. Look and see.

> *Blessed be the God and Father of our Lord Jesus Christ, who has blessed us in Christ with every spiritual blessing in the heavenly places, even as he chose us in him before the foundation of the world, that we should be holy and blameless before him. In love he predestined us for adoption to himself as sons through Jesus Christ, according to the purpose of his will, to the praise of his glorious grace, with which he has blessed us in the Beloved.*
>
> —Eph. 1:3–6

God's Word says I don't have to look through the gloomy lens of my old self. I can see everything clearly through the lens of the gospel. All my actions can flow from that truth. As a husband, I can treat my wife "according to the purpose of his will." As her lover and best friend, I can care for her and be intimate with her "to the praise of his glorious grace." Together we can raise "holy and blameless" kids in peace, in unity, and in harmony. I believe that is what should drive people to get married, the chance to serve a timeless purpose through a lifelong commitment to a spouse, a union that was designed by none other than God himself. So, men, when you stand at the altar, you should be in full confidence that you are carrying out God's will for your life. Ladies, when you walk down the aisle, it should be in full faith that the Lord is bringing you to your man (Gen. 2:22). This book can help you better understand how to get there, but most importantly I hope it shows you why you should get there.

Many people focus so much of their attention and efforts on *how* to gain a lifelong companion that they forget to consider the *why.* Instead of praying, *Lord, is it your will that I should be married?* they're asking themselves, *How can I hurry up and get married?* Then, after years of fighting, distance, and unhappiness, they reach a breaking point and start asking, *Lord, please get me out of this marriage.* Instead of asking, *Should I get married?* they automatically assume it's God's will for them too. If the relationship isn't strong enough, to begin with, it could cause irreconcilable differences. Then you end up asking, *How the heck did I ever marry this person?* The number of failed marriages in the United States has skyrocketed over the last few decades. Divorce and adultery were thought to be shocking and abominable long ago, but now they are quite common and come as no surprise. The faithful are quickly becoming faithless. Too many women are looking for that secret "guy on the side," while a lot of men are on the constant prowl for a "side chick."

Purity has become a thing of the past. Pornography is now praised, and piety seems obsolete. People have been marrying because of lust, not love, and now a lot of spouses feel stuck, even trapped. People are making decisions to stay together based on what's best for their kids and what spares the family name from embarrassment or shame. On the flip side, unmarried couples are simply moving in together. They think it's safer and less complicated. They consider what makes sense financially and dismiss altogether what makes sense biblically. More and more singles are avoiding the decree of marriage, preferring to live with no strings attached, as partners, or as friends with benefits. For those struggling with patience in finding a soulmate, the outlets are inappropriate dating sites and X-rated adult entertainment. Our culture thinks those outlets are somehow stepping stones in the pursuit of love and happiness.

At an increasing rate, even in the Christian community, some are dealing with same-sex attraction and redefining marriage as the union of two men or two women. It's easier for them to do so now that every US state allows same-sex marriage. These days, protecting human rights supersedes implementing godly standards and Christ-like principles. We have forgotten that marriage doesn't start with a bill of rights or with how we sexually identify ourselves. It doesn't start with a diamond ring or a temporary infatuation. It doesn't even start with *us* really. It starts with God. It starts with how *he* identifies us. It starts with how he designed and created us. The best way to pursue marriage is through objective truth contained in the Word of God—the Bible.

Allow me to pose these questions: Is your definition of marriage biblical, or is it solely based on how you feel? Does your idea of marriage run on emotion, or is it fueled by unwavering faith in the Lord? Here's a question all of us need to ask ourselves: Should it matter what God thinks about marriage? The answer is yes. In fact, the Bible in its entirety is the messy love story of *one* God forever united to *one* people. That *one* group of people is collectively called the Bride of Christ. The Scriptures tell the epic saga of God's triumph over all negative components that sabotage marriages, things like loneliness, separation, depression, abandonment, adultery, abuse, pride, and even death. You name it, the Lord has overcome it. The Bible is the testimony of God uniting us to him in perfect togetherness. He does this with true love—true love that lasts forever. How do we know? Because the Word tells us.

> Anyone who loves me will obey my teaching. My Father will love them, and we will come to them and make our home with them.
>
> —John 14:23 (NIV)

> As for you, see that what you heard from the beginning remains in you. If it does, you also will remain in the Son and in the Father. And this is what he promised us—eternal life.
>
> —1 John 2:24–25 (NIV)

All of life is lived in the midst of this unifying process. God's demonstration of faithfulness in Scripture and Jesus's example of humility apply to every area of our lives, including our marriages. Similar to how we as spouses set out to honor our commitments, God has set in motion a plan to honor his commitment to love us forever and live with us for all time. Once we discover this for ourselves in Scripture, we can better know and understand what it means to be a husband or a wife and what it means to be joined together in holy matrimony. There is a right way to do marriage. And the right way is meant to protect us from doing it the wrong way. Marriage relationships should be pursued through the guidance of the Holy Spirit and carried out reverently. My purpose in writing this book is so all husbands (myself included) and their

wives can be trained, equipped, and sent out into society with the
fidelity of God's spirit and the devotion of Jesus's heart. My goal is
for us to dig deeper into the meaning and purpose of our spousal
roles. By evaluating the areas where growth and refinement are
needed, we can become better servants. Wherever we lack clarity,
God's Word is our go-to guide for enlightenment. Whenever we
struggle, Jesus's words are our source of strength. Jesus said this:

> *Come to me, all who labor and are heavy laden, and I
> will give you rest. Take my yoke upon you, and learn
> from me, for I am gentle and lowly in heart, and you
> will find rest for your souls. For my yoke is easy, and
> my burden is light.*
>
> —Matt. 11:28–30

If we can motivate each other to add peace to our marriages
and fill them with God's love, we can together stand firm as
unified couples for Christ. If we can honor our vows on the firm
foundation of Jesus and hold fast to our spouses through faith, we
can participate in the furtherance of the gospel community with
Christ-like love. We can bring glory to God everywhere we go.
As you continue to turn each page of this book, you will embark
on a journey that is sure to make you a better friend, lover, and
companion. Let's get started.

Chapter 1

Marriage Is about God

I never believed in unconditional anything, let alone uncon-ditional love. For me, love fell under the rule of terms and conditions. That seemed to apply to everything else in life. If I behaved, I got rewarded. If I misbehaved, I got in trouble. If I did well in school, I got to pass to the next grade. If I performed well at work, I got to keep my job. The rule of terms and condi-tions seemed like the most logical principle to apply to love. If you love me, I'll love you back. If I do something out of love for you, I expect something in love back. If I am kind and cordial, I expect the same from you. When I was young and immature, that way of thinking made the most sense. So I treated others exactly how they treated me. If they were jerks to me, I was a jerk back. If they were cool, I was cool. If they hated me, I hated them. If they liked me, I liked them back. And only if they loved me first would they get to benefit from my love.

That changed when my firstborn son, Michael, came into the world. He arrived in the summer of 1997 at a difficult time in my life, much different than now. Back then I was coldhearted and cruel. I never cared for much of anything or anyone. But I remember the night Michael was born. It was amazing. That whole experience was surreal. The joy of holding my brand-new baby was unspeakable without a doubt. Michael had tiny little hands and tiny feet. I can recall his gorgeous eyes, soft skin, full head of hair, puffy cheeks, and bulbous nose. I was in awe, even of his perfect little fingernails. Looking at him, I knew my heart would never be the same.

Love at First Sight

Soon after Michael was delivered, I managed to quietly carry him to an adjacent room away from his mom and the midwife—just the two of us. As I held him, tears filled my eyes. He hadn't said a word or done anything, yet I knew I wanted to care for him, protect him, and be his dad until the day I died. In that father-son moment, I said to him, "I will love you my whole life." I meant it too. That was monumental for me. Up until that point in my life, I hadn't cared for anyone more than I cared for myself. I hadn't loved anyone more than I loved myself. Pretty crazy, huh? Before becoming a dad, I was apathetic to almost everything. I had no passion or drive. I wasn't living life; I was just existing through life. But then my newborn child made me think about things I'd never been interested in—things like purpose, meaningfulness, sacrificial love, and benevolence. There was a softening sensation in my heart that enabled me to give love without first receiving it. A mind shift took place that allowed me to put a child's life before my own.

That important perspective only increased when my second son, Nicholas, was born. Love at first sight struck again. It happened again with my third son, Ezra, and my fourth son, Jack.

There is clearly a naturally occurring emotional connection and an unbreakable bond between a dad and his boys. As it turns out, I'm not the only person who's ever felt that way. In fact, our society is no stranger to love at first sight. Other dads and moms have experienced it with their sons and daughters. Many husband-and-wife couples have also experienced it with each other. Our entire human history is filled with stories from generation to generation of the instantaneous animation of love. Yes, love at first sight is a more common experience than you might think. And it dates back to when the earth was first created. It's actually connected to the very first man to ever walk the earth—Adam.

After God created the first man, he proceeded to create Eve, the first woman on earth. When God introduced Adam to Eve, you can tell by Adam's response that he was more than pleased to make her acquaintance. Eve was the perfect representation of femininity and womanhood, and she did more than spark Adam's curiosity and interest. Adam was ecstatic when he saw her, beyond thrilled, and he instantaneously loved her.

> Then the man [Adam] said, "This at last is bone of my bones and flesh of my flesh; she shall be called Woman, because she was taken out of Man."
>
> —Gen. 2:23

Adam used the phrase "at last." It is emphasized because this moment occurred only after the daunting task of naming every member of the animal kingdom, which at the very least was a full day's work.

> [T]he LORD God had formed every beast . . . and every bird and brought them to the man to see what he would call them. And whatever the man called every living creature, that was its name. The man

> *gave names to all livestock and to the birds . . . and to*
> *every beast. . . . But for Adam there was not found a*
> *helper fit for him.*
>
> —Gen. 2:19–20

As every living creature poured into Adam's territory—the Garden of Eden—Adam clearly saw that the lioness was made for the lion, the doe for the buck, the cow for the bull, the ewe for the ram, and so on. Through this process, Adam learned more about his role as a man. He discovered his distinction from the roles of the animals since he possessed authority and dominion. Through his God-given leadership, the appropriate food chain would be established, and proper societal order would come to fruition. That made it easy for Adam to know that his classification of species was unique. A human's sex, gender, and identity, which we'll discuss throughout this book, were set apart from the birds and the bees, the flowers and the trees.

So when Eve finally showed up, Adam noticed immediately that she was his one and only companion—a helper fit for him, *at last*. As Adam gazed on her beautiful skin, her perfect body, her eyes, and her smile, his hope and joy were made complete by his other half. God intended this to be a romantic occasion, a cherishable surprise, one that Adam would hold dear. Imagine falling asleep alone—like Adam did—and then waking up with the perfect soulmate by your side. You're in the middle of paradise together, completely naked, and the whole world is yours. This is the stuff dreams are made of—pure bliss in the morning, afternoon delight, and never-ending nights of passion. But this perfect world was no fantasy. It was reality for Adam and Eve. It was the inaugural perfect union of true love between man and woman that God himself singlehandedly designed. We call it marriage.

Although things went awry in the Garden of Eden where the world's earliest marital problems took place, the pursuit of marriage continues today. We will talk more about the successes of marriage and the struggles of the institute of marriage in the chapters to come. But for now, let's further explore this concept of love at first sight. Here's why. It's because love at first sight initiates more than giddy couples and love-struck parents. And we don't have to be searching for a lifelong partner or expecting a child to experience it. Love at first sight correspondingly hits us the day we give our lives to Christ. When we confess with our mouths that Jesus is Lord and believe in our hearts that God sent him to bring us eternal life, we are saved. That instance is special, and God's love remains unlike any other.

Love at First Light

When God came into my life, I entered into an immediate permanent relationship with Jesus. It honestly felt like connecting with a long-lost love. It was like I knew him but had been distancing myself from him. I was running away from him with cold feet, leaving him at the altar, if you will. When God poured his love into my heart, it felt like new love. But since he had been drawing me to him, it also felt familiar. It was like a reconciling type of love that filled a void in my life that only he could satisfy. It was as if he'd planted a seed in my heart and then faithfully watered it year after year. Season after season he patiently waited to finally give it growth. I know now that's what he was doing all along. I just didn't have eyes to see him working behind the scenes. A veil was covering my heart. But when the veil was lifted, "at last" the Savior's love set me free. I know now that was his master plan the entire time. Long before I was even born, God's will to love me and for me to love him was waiting.

And the same is true for every believer—every Christian. God's love for all his people precedes time and transcends space.

> *For he chose us in him before the creation of the world to be holy and blameless in his sight. In love he predestined us for adoption to sonship through Jesus Christ, in accordance with his pleasure and will.*
>
> —Eph. 1:4–5 (NIV)

Before the beginning of time, God was making decisions that pertained to our relationship with him. Did you know that? Did you know that before you even existed, God had a plan to love you unconditionally? God designed his church to be a people loved by him through the perfect love of Jesus. Our relationship with God is the most important thing to him on this planet, even more important than the sun, moon, and stars. Every Christian man and woman, husband and wife, holds more value to him than all creation. God's love for his people will always be greater than anything he has made. As the years go by, the climate will change, natural resources will further deplete, environmental concerns will arise, and our planet will inevitably become an unlivable place—an uninhabitable hothouse. But because God's love will always be, rest assured that his people will live on. Every member of the Bride of Christ will be protected by an impenetrable union of togetherness. For all of God's children, there will be no reason to fear separation or a decree of dissolution. His Word confirms that the love he has for us overcomes everything.

> *Love bears all things, believes all things, hopes all things, endures all things. Love never ends.*
>
> —1 Cor. 13:7–8

God's love is endless, and it's always been that way. Isn't it amazing how thousands of years ago, God had *us* on his mind and in his heart? Isn't it comforting to know that he cares about us more than the earth, the solar system, and our galaxy? He loves us beyond the deepest unknown corners of outer space. Speaking of the cosmos, did you know our universe was quite different at the beginning of time? It was nothing like we know it today. There was no sound as we know it, no taste, nothing visible, and nothing to feel. There was no sun, no stars, no moon, no sky—only darkness. Then, in one instant, God initiated creation. And just like that, at the sound of God's voice, out of nothing, everything came to be. All God had to do was speak, and thin air yielded to his command.

> *And God said, "Let there be light," and there was light.*
> —Gen. 1:3

No one else has the power to do something like this. Light didn't happen by chance or accident. When God made the decision to "let there be light," he alone provided the opportunity for billions upon billions of men and women to live and love, and that includes me and you. Without light, there is no experience of life. Without life, there is no experience of love. And because God predestined us in love before we were created—prior to there being light—we can be sure his decision was made out of unconditional love. If we could have somehow watched creation unfold, we would have seen that God spoke everything into existence out of his love for us to live. Scripture confirms this:

> *Give thanks to the LORD, for he is good, for his steadfast **love** endures forever. . . . to him who alone does great wonders . . . his steadfast love endures*

> *forever; to him who by understanding made the heavens . . . to him who spread out the earth above the waters . . . his steadfast love endures forever; to him who made the great lights . . . the sun to rule over the day . . . the moon and stars to rule over the night . . . his steadfast love endures forever.*
>
> —Ps. 136:1–9

Everything good, everything grand, all of infinite space, God made it all out of love. Everything we know as pleasurable, all sustenance, comfort, and shelter, was most definitely created out of love. Everything that causes us to marvel, everything amazing, everything far out and incredible, super, and extraordinary are connected to the unsurpassed creativity of God. This unsurpassed creativity originates from his infinitely loving mind. So you see, the more we learn about God's perfectly prodigious love, the better loving men and women we can be. The deeper knowledge we have concerning God's wondrously unfailing love, the more capable we are of being loving husbands and wives. Love is the ultimate motive for sharing life together, the most powerful source for couples, and the most fundamental component of marriage. But to comprehend God's reason for marriage, God's plan for spousal roles, and God's goal with intimacy, we must first understand God's purpose in creation.

Marriage Begins with God

So why did God create us? I believe it was out of love. But we'll have to ask him that when we get to heaven. Add that to the many inquiries into God's mysterious will. As we live and breathe, we're always going to have questions about God. That's part of what makes him God—our inability to fully comprehend him. But it isn't that he wants us to be clueless. God didn't just throw us on this planet and say, "Okay, now figure it out." No, he reveals himself to us in a manner that we can draw near to him and know him. But why do we need to know God? Why do we need to draw near to him? Those are loaded questions yet so easy to answer when you think about them.

Look at it this way. If you are already married, take a minute to think about the day you met your spouse and the time leading up to your wedding day. It could be days, weeks, months, years—however long. If you're engaged, take a minute to think about your fiancé from the moment you met each other until now. Or if you're currently single, take a minute to think about someone of the opposite sex—a friend or significant other, for example, that you could see yourself marrying someday. Now picture yourself at the altar. Picture yourself standing next to the person you are going to spend the rest of your life with. Picture yourself making a lifelong commitment to the person you will be sleeping with, waking up next to, eating with, raising kids with, vacationing with, going through tough times with, and celebrating with. It's the same person you will be looking to for deep comfort, ongoing communication, guidance, and counsel for the rest of your life.

Is that person a complete stranger, or have you gotten to know them? Of course, you've gotten to know them. Is that person distant from you, or have you drawn near to them? Of course, you've drawn near to them. You most likely have full confidence in that person and are in love with them. Shouldn't you love them before committing the rest of your life to them? Of course, you should love and trust them. If you can picture yourself exchanging vows with that person publicly, in front of all your friends and family, isn't that the result of drawing near to them? Isn't that a sign that you've reached a level of closeness strong enough for them to be a huge part of your life? Of course, it is. Well, it's the same with God. The better we know him, the closer we get to him. The closer we get to him, the stronger our relationship becomes with him. The stronger our relationship is with him, the more we can navigate through life toward his will, which is his best for our good and the good of our marriage.

When I met my wife, Brittany, I was positive that we were just going to be friends. I thought she was very gorgeous and I found her to be extremely attractive, but then, love was just a game to me. In my mind, the pursuit of marriage was a survival of the fittest. It was all about which woman could be the most fun, the most satisfying, the least confrontational, and the least restrictive. I didn't think Brittany fit the bill, so I friend-zoned her. She was too quiet and seemed unsure of herself. She had a resting-mean-face and didn't look happy at all. She never smiled. But then one day I said something to her that made her smile. Her face lit up, and she looked like a completely different person. As we occasionally spoke to one another, I found myself wanting to spend more time with her. So I asked her out. I'm glad I did because it ended up being the most memorable first date I had ever had. By the end of that night, I had learned so much about her. But it wasn't enough. I wanted more. A few nights later, I took her to dinner.

Things went well from that point on, but it was still a game to me. I ended up treating Brittany as an alternate who had a winning chance. I treated her like an option, an escape, a break from the pressures of having to impress women. Back then, I obsessed daily with saying all the right things, wearing all the right clothes, and acting right in front of women. I didn't think of Brittany like that. She was my divergent girl. I could relax and be myself around her. She loved that. I loved that. That's how we became best friends. But things were brewing a little differently in Brittany's mind. You see, she had been praying and waiting for God to steer her in the direction of true, lifelong love. She was being led by the Holy

Spirit to what she believed was marriage material—namely, me. As she observed me and got to know me, the question in her head became, *Really, God? This guy?* Even though I wasn't fitting the bill, Brittany never once put me on the back burner. She trusted God, drew closer to him, and as a result, God drew the two of us closer. Monday through Friday we saw each other and did stuff together. In faith, Brittany left her church of 15 years and joined mine. Now I was with her on Sundays too. Months went by, and all *my* friends quickly became *her* friends to the point where they'd say things like, "Dude, what about Brittany?" I still wasn't seeing it, not until one Sunday morning during worship.

If you've ever gone to a contemporary church service, you know they typically start with a praise and worship band leading the congregation in a few songs before the sermon. So there Brittany and I were, singing to God, eyes closed, with our hands lifted up. Then suddenly, I noticed something I had never noticed before. Brittany has a beautiful voice. I couldn't help but open my eyes to look over at her. There she stood, pouring her heart out in praise, singing at the top of her lungs about Jesus's victory and triumph over death. Wow! It was beautiful. It reminded me of how zealous I used to be as a new Christian. At that moment I realized I'd lost some fire in my faith. I knew I was a believer, but I surely wasn't living up to it. Then a voice went off in my head as I watched Brittany, and this is what I heard: *You are so blind. Every day you rack your brain searching, hoping, begging for the right woman to show up in your life when this whole time she's been right before your very eyes.*

To this day, I believe God was speaking. I'm not an expert on what the voice of God sounds like, but here's what I heard next. *Marriage doesn't begin with you; it begins with me. Your heart can never decide what's best for you, but I can, not just in this life but also in the next. Face it, you've been spiraling out of control farther and farther away from me, and if you're not careful, you'll lead Brittany astray. I brought you this woman. I gave you this daughter of mine so that together the two of you could be one in your pursuit of me.*

When I heard, "pursuit of me," it was like a light bulb went off in my head. That's how I felt at that moment. I knew God had a plan for me to be a better man and a better father. I knew he wanted me to have a second chance at being a husband and becoming a stronger leader. What I didn't know was that plan would never unfold without my other half—Brittany.

Marriage Begins with God's Glory

In my case, God's reason for marriage was connected to a bigger picture. God brought marriage into my life to produce purity— to redirect my heart, mind, and soul toward faithfulness and fidelity. But most important, it was to show me I knew very little about love. Even though I had been in serious relationships time and time again, I knew more about *lust* than *love*. Even though I had been married once before, I knew more about loving myself than about loving a spouse. Even after bringing children into this world, I knew more about taking care of myself than taking care of my loved ones. That's sad, isn't it? Here's the reason it's sad. The elements of a good marriage have nothing to do with lust, and the traits of a good husband far exceed his concern for himself.

The plan for spousal roles was never supposed to be for selfish gain. It's supposed to produce unifying companionship in the Lord. The joining of a man and a woman to become husband and wife was never meant for shame. It is meant for glory. Glory is going public and manifesting something that catalyzes a widespread effect. We all understand glory, yet it's an old-fashioned word that people hardly use anymore. I wish we would bring it back because there should be glory in marriage. And since God designed marriage, the glory should always start with him.

> *Ascribe to the LORD the glory due his name; worship the LORD in the splendor of holiness . . . The voice of the LORD is powerful; the voice of the LORD is full of majesty . . . The LORD sits enthroned as king forever.*
>
> —Ps. 29:2–10

Never forget God's glorious words for us— "Let there be light." And remember, without light, there is no experience of life. Without life, there is no experience of love. And without love, there is no ultimate motive for marriage. These fundamental truths are what help us when relationships get tough. They are the foundation that withstands struggle and difficulty. They can bring peace to a domestic dispute. If you're ever on the verge of breaking up or calling it quits, fundamental truths can help you reason with your spouse to make peace.

It should humble you to know that your very life, your entire existence, is at the mercy of God's voice. Tomorrow—tonight even—God could decide, "Let there be nothing," and all of creation would have to obey. Or if he said, "Let it all be over," none of us would be able to live on. We know that God is a loving God and that it's completely unlikely he would do something like that. At the same time, he could if he wanted to. After all, he is God. But we know that he would rather make peace. According to his Word, we know there is more glory in life than in death. There is more glory in rescue than in abandonment.

> *For God so loved the world, that he gave his only Son, that whoever believes in him should not perish but have eternal life.*
>
> —John 3:16

In marriage, there is more glory in hearts that join together than there ever will be in hearts that cause division. There is more glory in love that unifies than there ever will be in hate that splits people up. The only thing hate produces is ruin. So we are better off being husbands and wives on the side of life and love.

Most of us know what it's like to experience loss. For example, we know what it's like when people's lives end abruptly. If you've ever had a loved one who was gone too soon or a friend who left this earth prematurely, you understand grief at its most confusing and painful level. We don't get to decide when our time is up, but we *can* decide what we do with the time we get. Here's my point: God has given us life and therefore has given us love. So while we're alive, we should make the most of life and the most of love. Can you imagine leaving this world on bad terms? Think about the most recent conflict you had with your spouse, fiancé, or significant other. What if what you said during that conflict were your last words on earth? Would it have communicated life and love, or would it have resembled something negative? Here's a more important question: Would it have been glorifying to God?

Why is that the more important question? Because glory is God's purpose in creation. The glory of the Father, the glory of the Son, and the glory of the Holy Spirit are all going public, manifesting the holiness of God.

> *Holy, holy, holy is the LORD Almighty; the earth is full of his glory.*
>
> —Isa. 6:3

This truth is relevant to husbands and wives since marriage is often referred to as holy matrimony. Spousal roles are one of the ways God's glories are displayed throughout the world.

When Brittany and I got married, our union was a joining of two separate paths in pursuit of one goal—the glory of God through faith. And now, everything we do is connected to that end. We believe our love is a testimony to those around us, a testimony of God's love. We believe everyone who possesses God's love testifies to the ongoing story of redemption to others. All marriages reveal God's blessing of intimacy and grace. Intimacy is what you feel physically and spiritually when love is at work. It is one of the products of love. When the love of God is at work, his people know it, his children feel it, and his church experiences it. That is God's glory in consummation. And our goal should be that every marriage, all relationships, be centered on the glory of God.

It seems fitting that every man and every woman, all created by God, define and pursue love through the definition and pursuit of God's glory. This is biblical—it is Christ-like. It is the way of all Christians, no matter if they're married, engaged, or single. Listen to the voice of Paul the Apostle when he poured out love to his family and friends in the Church of Philippi.

> *It is right for me to feel this way about you . . . because I hold you in my heart, for you are all partakers with me of grace . . . in the defense and confirmation of the gospel. For God is my witness, how I yearn for you all with the affection of Christ Jesus. And it is my prayer that your love may abound . . . so that you may approve what is excellent, and so be pure and blameless for the day of Christ, filled with the fruit of righteousness . . . to the glory and praise of God.*
> —Phil. 1:7–11

Every Christian should hold the family of God dear in their hearts. In marriage, that mindset enables us to yearn for our spouses with the affection of Jesus. Our marital love should be an extension of the unconditional love God provides for us. It should resemble the sacrificial love of Christ that is available to us and the Holy Spirit's unifying love that dwells within us. Marital love that is filled with the fruit of righteousness flows down the path to the chief end of humankind, which is to glorify God and enjoy him forever.

Chapter 2

Jesus Is Our Example

God is in the business of cultivating life. And because he is a benevolent God, he sustains and upholds life with love. Everyone who draws near to God regards life with the utmost honor, respect, and sincerity. No one did this better than Jesus. No one regarded the sanctity of human life more than Jesus. His knowledge of love is unparalleled to this day. His understanding of the value of men and women will forever remain unmatched. Our Savior once said this:

> *Greater love has no one than this, that someone lay down his life for his friends.*
>
> —John 15:13

Jesus fully comprehends the business of sustaining and upholding life with love. If there is anyone who should instruct us on marriage, it is Jesus. Here's one reason why:

> *A new commandment I give to you, that you love one another: just as I have loved you, you also are to love one another. By this all people will know that you are my disciples, if you have love for one another.*
>
> —John 13:34–35

These verses from the Gospel of John are direct quotes from Jesus. They are words in the history of the greatest man who ever lived and evidence of his extraordinary example. When it comes to lifelong love, we can trust Jesus for guidance. A lot of what he says can be applied to our marriages. In this chapter, we'll be taking a close look at some of Jesus's words in John's Gospel. There will be a few paragraphs on theology, along with a snippet of my own biblical convictions and personal history. But first, here's another direct quote from Jesus:

> *For this purpose I was born and for this purpose I have come into the world—to bear witness to the truth. Everyone who is of the truth listens to my voice.*
>
> —John 18:37

After reading that verse, ask yourself this question: "Am I of the truth?" If you are of the truth, according to Jesus you will listen to his voice. How awesome is that? Simply by being a believer, you can listen to the Son of God. You can understand and adhere to the voice of Jesus. Simply by being a husband or wife of the truth, you can receive divine counsel and heavenly help to strengthen your marriage. That's good news because you'll definitely need it.

Jesus Teaches Us to Love

Every couple is led by an imperfect leader. All imperfect leaders make mistakes. They all break promises, they all lose their tempers, and they've all said and done things they wish they could take back. There is only one perfect leader, only one perfect person, and that's Jesus. Because of that, you cannot rely on your spouse to mend your imperfect marriage. That would be a futile pursuit. The perfect solution to ease spousal differences is to draw near to God. Having constant faith to clothe yourself in Jesus's humility helps bring perfect resolution to marital conflict. Growing in godliness is a quest that leads to tranquility and peace.

> *Thus, says the LORD: "Stand by the roads, and look, and ask for the ancient paths, where the good way is; and walk in it, and find rest for your souls."*
>
> —Jer. 6:16

No one in all of history walked down a better path than Jesus did. Many of us strive daily to ensure we achieve our full potential. Meanwhile, Jesus defined full potential. I once thought, *If Jesus is such a great example for us to emulate, why didn't he get married?* I told myself, *What a perfect opportunity Jesus had while here on earth to model the perfect spouse and perfect marriage.* Well, the fact is that he did all of that and more. Figuratively speaking, *we* are his bride, and *he* is our bridegroom. The Word of God tells us this:

> *Let us rejoice and exult and give him glory, for the marriage of the Lamb has come, and his Bride has made herself ready; it was granted her to clothe herself with fine linen, bright and pure—for the fine linen is the righteous deeds of the saints.*
>
> —Rev. 19:7–8

This is difficult for us to understand, but make no mistake, it is true. In Revelation 19:7, we read that for the Lamb—Jesus—his marriage has come. His Bride, more commonly known as the Body of Christ, is the church—all believers. The church makes up the body, and the body is the bride. We Christians are that bride. This verse goes on to say that we have made ourselves ready. But ready for what? Paul tells us *what* in his letter to the Ephesian church.

> *[S]o that [Jesus] might present the [bride] to himself in splendor, without spot or wrinkle or any such thing, that she might be holy and without blemish.*
>
> —Eph. 5:27

How do we make ourselves ready for this presentation? It is granted to us through the gift of God—our faith—and the righteous deeds that correlate with us being saints led by the Holy Spirit. You see, when we become Christians, that conversion produces in us an irresistible appetency to live like Jesus lived—to love sacrificially. Then, when we marry, we become Christian husbands and wives. Living how Jesus lived—holy and without blemish—teaches us to love sacrificially. And if Jesus demonstrated the greatest love by laying down his life for his friends, we can demonstrate great love by laying down our lives for our spouses. We probably won't ever have to literally die for our spouses as Jesus died for us, but there are many ways we can lay down our lives and die to ourselves.

For example, we can lay down our pride to become humble husbands and wives. We can lay down our anger to become more peaceful couples. We can make lifestyle changes; we can spend more time at home together. We can do more things one on one with our spouses. We can turn our coveted "me time" into "us time." For those of you who want to start families, you can lay down your dreams and ambitions to create time and space for children. When you lay down your life for the sake of your marriage, you communicate genuine care and authentic love to your spouse. That sets a Christ-like example and brings glory to God.

Love is how all people will know that we are his disciples. Love shows the whole world who we are in Christ. That is amazing to me. What an extraordinary concept! Jesus could have given any new commandment for us to live by. He could have said, "Work hard as I have worked hard" or "Don't give up as I never gave up, and don't quit as I never quit." He could have said, "Be successful as I have been successful." Jesus knew that none of those principles would be fitting enough to fully honor God. Grit and grind alone don't make you holy and without blemish. You need authentic love. That is to say, you need the Holy Spirit to enter your heart and teach you the truth. You also need sacrificial love, and Jesus is the embodiment of sacrificial love. Finally, you need unconditional love, which can only be found in God because God *is* unconditional love (1 John 4:8).

Before becoming a Christian, my heart was filled with a lot of hate. So I was excited to replace my hate with the love of Jesus toward others. In my marriage today, the command to love as Jesus loved us helps me love my wife. Had it not been for the love of Jesus, Brittany and I wouldn't be together anymore. We really struggled our first year. We were frequently at odds with each other. I was too immature to see certain things like how much of a flirt I was. I never considered Brittany's perspective on that. I thought I was better than her in all areas of life, so I never encouraged her to give me advice. That put distance between us. It jeopardized the foundation of our marriage, which had begun to crack. I needed help to be a better husband, and I found it in the words of Jesus.

Jesus Shows Us How to Live

I think of the Bible as the instruction manual for all things that pertain to life and love. Whenever I have questions or when I need guidance, the Word of God is where I enjoy going. Opening my Bible is like sitting down and starting a conversation with Jesus. The Word speaks in many wonderful ways to the entire Body of Christ. It is our guide to knowing what to think and how to act. The more we read God's Word, the more we get to know Jesus. The more we get to know Jesus, the stronger our faith is. The stronger our faith is, the more confidence we have in God's grace. The more confident we are in God's grace, the better off we are in times of need. If we want our marriages to last a life-time, we will need endless love alongside endless grace.

The Book of John is filled with testimony of Jesus's endless love and God's endless grace. I want to share with you my thoughts on a couple of events that John talked about in his Gospel regarding that. Those events happened during Jesus's missionary journey. They speak to us about how men should treat women, and vice versa. The first event we'll look at took place during a wedding at Cana in Galilee. It's when Jesus turned water into wine. But the miracle isn't what we'll focus our attention on. We'll actually be taking a close look at the dialogue between Jesus and his mother, Mary. They were both at the wedding. His disciples were there too. It was a big celebration with lots of people in attendance. During the dinner, Mary noticed that the wine for the reception was about to run out. She knew that Jesus could help out in the situation. Here's what happened.

> [A] marriage took place . . . and the mother of Jesus
> was there. . . . Jesus and his disciples were also invited.
> . . . And being short of wine, the mother of Jesus said

> *to him, "They have no wine." Jesus said to her, "What*
> *is that to me and you, woman? My hour has not yet*
> *come." His mother said to the servants, "Whatever he*
> *says to you, do."*
>
> —John 2:1–5 (ILB)

After that, Jesus instructed the servants to pour gallons and gallons of water into some tall, very large jars. The water was then taken to the father of the bride, and by the time he took a taste, it had transformed into the best wine he'd ever had. Impressed by this and assuming the newlywed groom was responsible, the father complimented him for providing beyond expectations. But the servants knew it was Jesus who deserved the credit, and so did Mary and the disciples. John tells us the point of this story.

> *What Jesus did here in Cana of Galilee was the first of*
> *his signs through which he revealed his glory; and his*
> *disciples believed in him.*
>
> —John 2:11

If you read this passage over and over, you'll find evidence of something deeper going on here. You must look past the surface to see it. The details John includes and the way he describes this occurrence reveal symbolic indications through this miracle. But never mind that for now. Let's discuss the obvious facts. Mary was concerned that the people responsible for providing wine would potentially suffer significant embarrassment—even consequences—if they ran out. She looked to Jesus to prevent that from happening. The way Jesus responded informs us that her request was untimely, so it caused tension between the two of them. Mary wanted him to take action, but his "hour has not yet come." The verbiage Jesus used tells us that it wasn't the appropriate time to publicly draw attention to himself. In fact, it communicated that if he had stood up and performed a miracle out in the open, something that wasn't good might have happened to him, which would have been far worse than the wine running out.

Jesus had a schedule by which he was carrying out his divine agenda. And Mary, being a hospitable mom, quick to assist others in need, wanted to help out so the celebration could continue. What we have here is a difference in priorities that created a slightly uncomfortable distance between Jesus and Mary. But her instructions inform us that Jesus and Mary were able to get on the same page.

> *His mother [Mary] said to the servants, "Whatever [Jesus] says to you, do."*
>
> —John 2:5 (ILB)

Mary knew it wasn't that Jesus *couldn't* help with providing more wine; it was that he needed to do it behind the scenes. Jesus saw a missional opportunity here and made the decision to act on it. He saw a divine appointment to honor his mother by granting her request but also for his disciples to witness the miracles he was capable of, all without interrupting his master plan or perfect schedule. This beautiful moment displays what the people of God can accomplish when they are led by his Son, Jesus. It's a demonstration of Jesus's power and what he achieved by showing the utmost honor, respect, and sincerity. At the wedding, Jesus honored God the Father by bringing him glory, to the benefit of his disciples. They believed in him, and their faith flourished. Jesus also honored his mother by having compassion for her and meeting the needs of the people she cared about.

There is a lot in this passage we can learn and apply to our marriages. Here are a few questions that will help.

- Husbands, do you honor your wife's requests even when they seem untimely?
- Wives, how do you respond when you and your husband aren't on the same page?
- Do either of you ever pressure each other into doing things?
- How confident are you in following each other's lead?
- Do you both strive to be on the same page together?

In marriage, spouses are not going to see eye to eye on everything. There will be times when your moods are out of sync. You'll misunderstand each other and butt heads. The main thing to remember is to stay on a mission for God. I often hear this saying: "You can tell how a man will treat his wife by the way he treats his mother." There is some truth to that. Here is one Bible verse that came to my mind when I was studying this passage.

Honor your father and your mother.
—Exod. 20:12

Scripture also says that when a man gets married, he shall leave his father and his mother and hold fast to his wife, and they shall become one flesh (Gen. 2:24). One implication here is that by the time a man moves out of his parent's house, he has been instructed on how women are to be treated. He is ready to move from under the authority of his mother to leading and loving his wife. Any man preparing for marriage should observe how he treats his mom, sister, aunt, and grandma. He should pay attention to how he treats women in general. From this perspective, there is a connection between how you honor your mother and how you honor your wife.

When I was single, my mom and I couldn't stand each other. I struggled to get along with her because she didn't approve of my lifestyle. I had very little respect for her authority, which made it easy for her to resent me. I treated my mom with severe disdain. My wife, Brittany, had no clue what to expect regarding how I would treat her because I resorted back to the rule of terms and conditions. And because I lacked unconditional love, I said things to my mom that I'm not proud of. But somehow God was able to soften my heart. Through his Word, I started paying attention to Mary's instruction in John 2:5, "His mother said to the servants, 'Whatever [Jesus] says to you, do.'"

During my season of singleness, I ignored a lot of what Jesus said to do. I was living a lie and thought of myself as a king, not a servant. I carried that lie with me into my marriage, and it brought my wife pain. I was distracted by my own selfishness, and it caused Brittany to cry a bucket of tears. I look back and think to myself, *What a fool. If I'd only paid more attention to what Jesus says to do.* I don't wish that kind of regret on any husband or wife. I encourage spouses to always look to Jesus as their example of leadership and honor. Whatever your situation, if you're following Jesus's example, the Holy Spirit will navigate you through it. He will always guide husbands and wives to what best honors God. Following Jesus is easier said than done. Trust me, I know it's tough. But it will always be the right thing to do.

Also, from this passage in John 2, you can look to Mary as an example of helping others. Getting on the same page with Jesus's words enabled her to participate in God's miraculous work. And look at the wedding servants. They are your reminder to follow through with whatever it is Jesus tells you to do. Leading, honoring, helping, and serving are what genuine devotion looks like. Genuine devotion leads to authentic love. Authentic love strengthens your relationship with your spouse and brings closeness. It will ease tension with comfort and peace. And as your devotion to your marriage produces peace, it will inspire those around you. It has the potential to change them as well.

Be Followers of Christ

The next event we'll look at took place at a water well in Samaria. Jesus is farther along on his missionary journey, and it's a completely different setting and situation. There is no crowd of people, no wine, and no miracles. It's the middle of the day, and the scorching sun is beating down on Jesus. He's hot, tired, and thirsty. Jesus's disciples have gone into town for groceries, so he is sitting at the well by himself. But he's not alone for long.

> *There came a woman from Samaria to draw water. Jesus said to her, "Give me a drink."... The Samaritan woman said to him, "How is it that you, a Jew, ask for a drink from me, a woman of Samaria?" (For Jews have no dealings with Samaritans.) Jesus answered her, "If you knew the gift of God, and who it is that is saying to you, 'Give me a drink,' you would have asked him, and he would have given you living water." The woman said to him, "Sir, you have nothing to draw water with, and the well is deep. Where do you get that living water? Are you greater than our father Jacob? He gave us the well and drank from it himself, as did his sons and his livestock." Jesus said to her, "Everyone who drinks of this water will be thirsty again, but whoever drinks of the water that I will give him will never be thirsty again. The water that I will give him will become in him a spring of water welling up to eternal life."*
>
> —John 4:7–14

A lot is going on at the start of this conversation, but what I would point out first is how unusual this interaction is. There were definitely chauvinistic men during Jesus's time, men who believed in not discussing theology with women. It was also traditionally known that Jews did not associate with Samaritans on the basis that they were "unclean." That was why the Samaritan woman was surprised that Jesus would even talk to her, let alone ask her for a drink. Here, Jesus rejects chauvinism by taking their conversation to a spiritual level. He responded graciously by hinting that he is the ultimate thirst quencher. Because of what the Samaritan woman says, we get the sense that she has pride in where she came from. She knows her roots and the religion of her people. But it also reveals that there is a significant amount of knowledge and truth she was lacking. Her life was incomplete, and Jesus showed up as her missing piece.

It is at this point in their dialogue that we can conclude a couple of things. First, men are never to be chauvinistic; chauvinism precludes the work of God. So husbands, be ready to have spiritual conversations with your wives and talk theology with them. Men and women equally need to hear the gospel and therefore equally serve as messengers of it. Our roles are different for sure, but in no way does that make either gender superior to the other. The second thing is this: We must know and understand the gift of God. Simply put, the gift of God is grace upon grace—grace and truth through his Son, Jesus (John 1:16–17). That's what was going on here—Jesus, a male Jew, was giving grace upon grace and speaking truth to a person who was not of the same sex or race. He was giving grace upon grace and speaking truth to a person of a different culture and belief system. Essentially, he was evangelizing a woman who was in desperate need of something more fulfilling than what this world had offered her.

The woman said to him, "Sir, give me this water, so that I will not be thirsty or have to come here to draw water." Jesus said to her, "Go, call your husband, and come here." The woman answered him, "I have no husband." Jesus said to her, "You are right in saying, 'I have no husband'; for you have had five husbands, and the one you now have is not your husband. What you have said is true."

—John 4:16–18

This Samaritan woman had gone from marriage to marriage searching for a life of happiness and peace. It doesn't sound like she'd found it yet. So Jesus opened a doorway to her heart and let her know that the only way she could find peace was through him. I love the connection that Jesus makes here to her past and her current relationship status. From her true response, we know she had integrity by not lying to him about her live-in boyfriend. She became curious about Jesus's faith and began thinking beyond the physical realm and into the spiritual realm.

The woman said to him, "Sir, I perceive that you are a prophet. Our fathers worshiped on this mountain, but you say that in Jerusalem is the place where people ought to worship." Jesus said to her, "Woman, believe me, the hour is coming when neither on this mountain nor in Jerusalem will you worship the Father. You worship what you do not know; we worship what we know, for salvation is from the Jews. But the hour is coming, and is now here, when the true worshipers will worship the Father in spirit and truth, for the Father is seeking such people to worship him. God is spirit, and those who worship him must worship in spirit and truth."

—John 4:19–24

Jesus let the Samaritan woman know her religion was pretty much insufficient. She couldn't just stare up into the spiritual realm with a moral liturgy and hope one day it would stare back and speak. She needed saving faith. Her soul needed to be informed with specifics. Her religion had to be built on a complete foundation of biblical truth. So Jesus let her in on who God really is. This endearing story reminds me of this psalm:

> You [God] have said, "Seek my face." My heart says to you, "Your face, LORD do I seek."
>
> —Ps. 27:8

In life, seeking God's face is most important, and Jesus knows that—He *is* God's face. This Samaritan woman who was spiritually bankrupt ended up face-to-face with God in the flesh, positioned for grace upon grace. Notice how Jesus didn't interrogate her about why she had been married five times. There was no dialogue on whether she cheated, got divorced, or swindled her way from husband to husband. There's no mention of it because it wasn't the urgent matter at hand. The most pressing issue was her salvation. Jesus wasn't looking for an opportunity to judge a sinner; he was looking to save a sinner.

> *The woman said to him, "I know that Messiah is coming (he who is called Christ). When he comes, he will tell us all things." Jesus said to her, "I who speak to you am he." Just then his disciples came back. They marveled that he was talking with a woman, but no one said, "What do you seek?" or, "Why are you talking with her?" So the woman left her water jar and went away into town and said to the people, "Come,*

see a man who told me all that I ever did. Can this be the Christ?" They went out of the town and were coming to him.

—John 4:25–29

Be Messengers of Genuine Faith

Here is the most beautiful part of this passage. You see, it wasn't enough for the Samaritan woman to have superficial faith. It wasn't enough to simply know the history of her religion and the traditional places to go for a spiritual gathering. She needed to confess specifically what she believed. She said she knew the one who is called Christ is coming and that "when he comes, he will tell us all things." As I studied this, I had to pause and think about whether or not she truly believed in the Messiah. She hadn't been living like it. But then I realized the magnitude of what happened next. Jesus looked her in the eye and said, "I who speak to you am he." When that happened, the Samaritan woman went from being totally lost to undeniably found.

She went from being without a Savior to being of the truth because she listened to his voice. Instantly, her spiritual life became her highest priority. She left her precious water jar at the well and ran down the mountain to share her testimony with her community. We know she shared it, energized with passion because it had such an impact on the city that the people made the trip back with her. They went up the mountain to the well to hear the words of Jesus. This entire event echoes the words of the prophet Isaiah:

How beautiful on the mountains are the feet of those who bring good news, who proclaim peace, who bring good tidings, who proclaim salvation, who say to Zion, "Your God reigns!"

—Isa. 52:7 (NIV)

Here's what spouses can learn from John 4. We all understand how life gets busy and tough. We saw it at the beginning of this passage.

> *[J]esus, wearied as he was from his journey, was sitting beside the well.*
>
> —John 4:6

This occurrence started out with a tired, thirsty, worn-out man. But even in his fatigue, Jesus pressed on to meet the needs of others. That's how we spouses must be. It will look different for each husband and wife. For me, it looks like this. Instead of coming home from a long workday to plop down on the sofa and binge-watch TV shows, I should arrive ready to serve my wife and minister to her. When I walk in the front door, it should be with purpose and leadership—I should be prepared to give love, extend grace, and speak the truth. It won't always be phenomenal. In fact, most evenings are pretty mundane. But if I can show my wife dedication day after day, night after night, she will experience authentic love. If husbands and wives come home and show their spouses' devotion, they will experience sacrificial love. And if you can demonstrate a spiritual life that is informed and biblical, you will experience the unconditional love of God, or as Jesus put it, "a spring of living water welling up to eternal life" (John 4:14).

I really do believe that authentic love, sacrificial love, and unconditional love are the driving forces of marriages that last. When temptations are high and stress levels are through the roof, the deepest kinds of love are what we must resort to. But sometimes we just aren't able. Sometimes we focus too much on the here and now. It's easy to do since we're only human. A lot of our days are spent prioritizing schedules and work, bills, and finances, as well as catching up on everything we're behind on. By the end of the week, we just want to relax and be left alone. We become so distracted that we don't recognize God staring us in the face, ready to save us from our troubles. Can you relate to the Samaritan woman's unawareness? If you were confronted by Jesus, would you know who he is?

I know that some spouses struggle to hear God speaking. It's happened to me before. How many of us have attended a marriage conference, for example, without hearing a single word that God was saying? I know I have. How many of our spouses have gotten neglected by our careers, hobbies, and the busyness of life? Yep, I'm guilty of that. When we don't pay attention to the spiritual side of life, our souls suffer. We get thirstier and thirstier and run to things that don't quench. If you need to strengthen your marriage, drink the living water that Jesus provides. If you want to be an even better spouse, relate to the latter version of the Samaritan woman going forward. She dropped everything at once to make Jesus her highest priority. The saved Samaritan woman was quick to share the truth of her Savior, motivating people and leading them to Christ. She was deeply moved by his telling of all things. When you allow Jesus to tell you all things, he becomes the perfect solution to the greatest of your needs. When you do whatever he tells you to do, he empowers you to honor your marital commitments. When you drink from the fountain of living water, it prepares you for the ultimate wedding day when we will unite with Jesus forever and ever. Amen.

Chapter 3

The Holy Spirit Is Our Guide

I remember quite vividly the first pornographic video I ever watched. It was during my middle childhood when VHS tapes and VCRs were at the height of technology. It was a time when pornography was hard for a kid to come by, but that didn't stop me from searching. Nudity was something I was drawn to. As soon as I saw one naked actress, I wanted to see them all. The moment I saw sex in a magazine or on TV, it became something I wanted to see again and again. Years later as an adolescent, I was drawn to sensual intimacy. My definition of dating and relationships equaled the seeking and savoring of physical pleasure. Females became the object from which I could attain ongoing gratification and emotional satisfaction.

When I couldn't physically be with a girl, I substituted nude scenes from movies and magazines with nude photos. After years of looking at naked female bodies, that behavior did something to my mind. It altered my thought process and embedded a craving in my heart that dominated my soul. That's probably why I started having sex at the age of 15. I needed the real thing; fantasies weren't enough. But no matter how much porn I watched, no matter how much sex I had, one thing remained true—it was *never* enough. At no point in time was I ever 100 percent satisfied. On the contrary, I developed a sense of personal grossness. It came with a guilty conscience and a self-perceived dirtiness, especially after I started lying about my porn addiction. It was a personal despicability I lived with for quite some time.

My first marriage was doomed from the start because of my dirty mindset. You might be asking, *Why is he sharing all these details?* Well, honestly, I know these details will get your attention. And if you struggle with secret sin, getting your attention is necessary to help you deal with that garbage. Even if porn or immorality hasn't tainted your personal life, it could be tainting your spouse's life, which means it affects you too. And without change, secret sexual sin can negatively affect all your relationships. Your friends and family members, your spouses and kids, your church—they can all be plagued by sin that isn't dealt with.

Some Roads Are Dead Ends

Porn, the most rampant secret sin, ruins marriages. It deteriorates and consumes until there's nothing left. It knows no bounds. It's like an unstoppable force that creeps its way into our homes, offices, churches, schools, bathrooms, bedrooms, hotels, parking garages, gyms, and locker rooms—virtually, porn is everywhere.

But it won't be forever. It will be defeated. God promises that many times in the Bible. Here's one example.

> *So put to death the parts of your life that belong to the earth, such as sexual immorality, moral corruption, lust, evil desire, and greed (which is idolatry). The wrath of God is coming upon disobedient people because of these things.*
>
> —Col. 3:5–6 (CEB)

I thank God for being a God of rescue and deliverance. Without ever batting an eye, I gave in to my secret sin (knowing it was wrong). I wish I could say that God was knocking on the door of my heart and I was refusing to let him in, but I was so self-absorbed that I didn't even know what God knocking on the door of my heart would sound like. And I certainly wasn't living in the truth yet, so I wouldn't have been able to listen to his voice. During those days, I felt little remorse about the things I did that ruined my first marriage. But I did feel the full weight of the fear of getting caught. That fear doubled down on my anxiety and inevitably produced a monstrous stress that made me sick to my stomach. Yet still, I continued to willfully avoid consequences by lying and covering up my secret sins.

That weight of fear and anxiety was very overwhelming. It was like carrying around a load of bricks that got heavier and heavier every day. I couldn't enjoy life with a heavy burden like that. It was emotionally paralyzing; it crippled my mind. It made it hard to swim at the beach with my kids or have a good time with my friends. Being heavily burdened with fear and anxiety— or, as I call it, strapped to a backpack full of bricks—made it hard to enjoy things and lead a normal life. For a Christian husband, being strapped to a backpack full of bricks makes it difficult to run the race of faith and live on a mission. For the unsaved husband, which was me, it made it difficult to want to live at all. That's how I felt—unsaved, faithless, hopeless, and worthless. I wondered what the point was to live the rest of my life as a liar with no integrity. Oh, and by the way, I was in the Marines during all this—you know, the few, the proud. It was the military branch whose motto is *Semper Fi* ("always faithful"), the service members whose core values are honor, courage, and commitment. My behavior wasn't just marring my role as a husband; it was unbecoming of a United States Marine. It was what most people refer to as toxic masculinity.

Once I got caught, everything surfaced. My ex-wife found me out and said she'd had enough. Her only option was to take the kids and separate from me. I had forced her into misery. But since I couldn't feel remorse, this was my response to her leaving (listen to my then-distorted logic):

> Fine! Go! I don't need you! I'll find someone else who I don't have to hide things from. Someone who will give me the freedom to do what I want, who won't restrict me and force me to do things I don't want to . . . like go to church. I need someone who doesn't care so much about religion.

Here's the worst part. I said, "Only an idiot would allow a book to dictate the outcome of their life."

The types of books I was referring to were religious books. During my first marriage, I converted to my then-wife's religion since she was getting more involved with her church. The book I lugged around with me then was known as "the quad." It was comprised of the King James Bible, the Book of Mormon, the Doctrine and Covenants, and the Pearl of Great Price. The religion I was a member of used these books to teach their interpretation of spirituality through morality. They taught against smoking, alcohol consumption, and watching X-rated movies. As a result, I had to drink, smoke, and watch porn behind my wife's back. But I don't blame religion for my secret sin. I also don't blame my first wife for anything bad that happened. I'm fully aware that my divorce was my fault. Back then, I thought that letting *any* book govern my life was to subject myself to a sheltering bondage that would not allow me to be who I was meant to be.

Here's the problem with that theory. I had no clue who I was meant to be. If I did, I probably wouldn't have drunk and smoked so much or watched obscene amounts of porn. Once I was single again, there was no limit to my recklessness. Within months I went off the deep end. My addictions took a dangerous turn for the worse into the darkest of pits, a downward spiral that had no end until the night I hit rock bottom. That unforgettable night started when I was at a bar. Before long, I was wasted and slipped into a scary blackout. Hours later when I came out of it, I heard a knocking sound. But it wasn't God knocking on the door of my heart—nope, not yet. First, I had to deal with the highway patrolman who was knocking on my driver's side window. Barely awake and still drunk, I opened my eyes, and all I saw were red and blue lights flashing everywhere. There was oncoming traffic veering away from the scene the police had coned off. My vehicle was facing the wrong way in the middle of the road. I had no clue where I was, no clue how I got there, and no clue how some 18-wheeler truck hadn't smashed into me.

The highway patrolman knocked again and pulled on my door handle. "Sir, please," he said. "Turn off your vehicle, take the key out of the ignition, and unlock your door."

I did exactly as he told me to. Shortly after, I was up against his car guarded by two officers who administered a breathalyzer. They skipped the field sobriety test; it was obvious I wasn't sober. I blew a 0.16, which was twice the legal limit for blood alcohol content.

For this wrongdoing, there would be no avoiding consequences. The police read me my rights, handcuffed me, and took me to jail. Once they processed and fingerprinted me, they stripped off my steel-toed boots and put me in a detox tank. I spent the rest of the night lying on a cold, hard, concrete floor that reeked of urine. I didn't sleep a wink. I just stared at the ceiling and literally from rock bottom wondered, *How the heck did I end up here?* But the answer was plain to see. All I had to do was retrace my steps.

Heading in the Wrong Direction

This whole ordeal started because I wanted the freedom to do whatever I wanted. That's all my life was about—doing whatever I wanted, saying whatever I felt like saying, thinking whatever I felt like thinking—complete freedom. So how did pursuing freedom get me locked up behind bars in a jail cell? It's because life doesn't begin with *my* definition of freedom; it begins with God's. He knows freedom better than I ever will. My idea of freedom took me spiraling out of control on a path to nowhere. I wasn't being careful; I was being careless, and I almost lost everything and everyone. I know now that God should decide what's best for me in this life and in the next. He gave me this life so I could pursue freedom in him, but I was doing the total opposite. What I was pursuing was a distorted view of freedom, a warped version of it that the Bible speaks against.

> *It is for freedom that Christ has set us free. . . . You, my brothers and sisters, were called to be free. But do not use your freedom to indulge the flesh; rather, serve one another humbly in love. For the entire law is fulfilled in keeping this one command: "Love your neighbor as yourself."*
>
> —Gal. 5:1, 13–14 (NIV)

For every potential husband or wife, the true path to marriage doesn't start with the party life as I mistakenly thought. It doesn't start with figuring out what makes you happy. It starts with a willingness to serve one another humbly in love. The journey to a long-lived marriage doesn't start with a narcissistic view of self-love like I once had. It starts with learning to love your neighbor as yourself. The point is that freedom is meant to be exercised with love that flows outwardly, not inwardly. It starts with an attitude of giving, not getting, and it is in our giving that we then receive. You see, marriage doesn't begin by selecting the person you'd like to sleep with for the rest of your life. It's not to be motivated by financial security or convenience. It doesn't start with chemistry or physical attraction, although that's important. Marriage should be inspired by a desire to live out God's will. It starts with a humble readiness to follow God's direction and reflect his character. It starts by committing to serve God wholeheartedly with love and sacrifice. In short, it starts with being led by the Holy Spirit.

Making a U-Turn toward God

According to the Bible, the Holy Spirit's presence helped unify the first marriage long ago. His handiwork was key to the union of Adam and Eve and many other couples throughout human history. There is no one today who takes a stronger stance against failing marriages than the Holy Spirit. He is always available to help restore husbands and wives and point them toward success. There is nothing stronger on earth that can keep couples united than the power of the Holy Spirit. Marriage must begin with the Holy Spirit because life begins with the Holy Spirit.

> [T]he LORD God formed the man of dust from the ground and breathed into his nostrils the breath of life, and [Adam] became a living creature.
> —Gen. 2:7

What do I mean by that? Let's revisit what we already know of the Holy Spirit and what we believe his purpose is. As we discussed in Chapter 1, the glory of the Holy Spirit is steadily going public to manifest the holiness of God. He is the way God intimately proclaims himself to us in personal form. He expresses the inner drive and desire of God in creation—and in redemption—by communicating God to us. In Chapter 2, we talked about the need for authentic love, and how it is the Holy Spirit who enters our hearts, gives us the truth, and then navigates us through the lifestyle of God's ways. These are truths for every believer. The Holy Spirit has a specific purpose for all who are of the truth. He ensures that we listen to his voice, the voice of Jesus, who once said this:

> *If you love me, you will keep my commandments. And I will ask the Father, and he will give you another Helper, to be with you forever, even the Spirit of truth, whom the world cannot receive, because it neither sees him nor knows him. You know him, for he dwells with you and will be in you.*
> —John 14:15–17

When we make the decision to follow Jesus, our new spiritual life begins with the Holy Spirit. So it would seem that the Holy Spirit's purpose—in general— is to bring forth life. (Keep reading; trust me, this all pertains to your marriage.) In the first chapter of this book, I also mentioned that creation was initiated by God out of love for us to live. Let's revisit that by looking again at the start of everything.

> *In the beginning, God created the heavens and the earth. The earth was without form and void, and the darkness was over the face of the deep. And the Spirit of God was hovering over the face of the waters.*
> —Gen. 1:1–2

The power of the person of God, the Holy Spirit, was there, in the beginning, to carry out the work of God in response to his love for us to live. As God spoke, the Holy Spirit took action to make what was once without form and void into the world we know today. Every sunrise and sunset, every new moon and eclipse, every fish in the sea, every animal that roams, every mountain, every tree—God made it all through his life-giving Holy Spirit. The air we breathe, the water we drink, the food we eat—they are all created by God through the ministry of the Holy Spirit. Ministry is what takes place when heaven reaches down to earth to meet human needs for the glory of God. It was the ministry of the Holy Spirit that sprouted vegetation, plants, fruit, and seeds (Gen. 1:11–12). Through the work of Creator God, the Spirit of God brought life to earth. Hovering over all things, he served as the personal catalyst who set the world in motion, bringing form and order to the atmosphere. He brought purpose and fullness to the planet.

Characteristically, that is how the Holy Spirit works. When I look back on the night I spent in jail lying on that dirty, rock-bottom floor, I see a man who was characterless, unordered, purposeless, dark, and empty. But God later chose to "let there be light" in my life, and the gospel of Jesus (the truth) spoke purpose into my heart. He enabled me to listen to his voice. When I eventually became a believer, the Holy Spirit began hovering over my life. He brought fullness to my emptiness and set my Christian walk of faith in motion. The Holy Spirit promises he will see this lifelong journey to completion.

> In [Christ] you also, when you heard the word of truth, the gospel of your salvation, and believed in him, were sealed with the promised Holy Spirit, who is the guarantee of our inheritance until we acquire possession of it, to the praise of his glory.
>
> —Eph. 1:13–14

Marital Help Comes from God's Spirit

Every believer is sealed with the promised Holy Spirit. That means every believing husband and wife has the Holy Spirit hovering over their marriage. The Holy Spirit is with us through whatever we might face. He's ready to minister to things such as loneliness and brokenness. The Holy Spirit is inside us. He's prepared to help us battle things such as depression and hopelessness. He is there to bring fullness and strength. He is there so we don't forget the wedding vows we once spoke. He is there to bring us peace and love so we will honor the marital commitments we made. The best way for us to pursue marriage and understand more about its meaning is with the Holy Spirit as our guide. The first place he guides us to for success is Scripture—God's Word.

It's pretty ironic how long ago I swore off religious books, and now here I am encouraging you to be led by the Holy Spirit. But if we know God, we know that's exactly how his Spirit works. He softens the coldhearted and gets through to the hardheaded. He takes a low-life nothing (like me) and produces a new person in Christ. He finds the worst of sinners (like me) and turns them into born-again believers. He sees what is *not* good and provides the solution for what *is* good. In doing so, he makes life both perfectly complete and completely perfect. That is the logic behind marriage—to create a perfect union between man and woman that is perfectly unified in Christ. Scripture tells us that's been God's will since Adam and Eve.

> Then the LORD God said, "It is not good that the man should be alone; I will make him a helper fit for him."
> —Gen. 2:18

The creation of the *helper* completes the creation of man. Together a husband and a wife are one in purpose. Man and woman are the perfect manifestations of created life and love. The man would never be able to procreate without the woman, and vice versa. That means that only together can they be abundantly productive. This was especially important at the start of humankind.

> *And God blessed them. And God said to them, "Be fruitful and multiply and fill the earth and subdue it. . . ." And God saw everything that he had made, and behold, it was very good.*
> —Gen. 1:28, 31

Throughout this book, we will be referencing the union of Adam and Eve. Remember, they were the very first couple and the only couple to experience marriage before marital problems existed. However, they were also the cause of the world's first marital mishap. What we learn from their story is invaluable to the foundation of our marriages. They remind us of our need to stay in step with the Holy Spirit and of our dependence on the grace of God. A longstanding marriage is best built on biblical truth and best achieved by maintaining a godly perspective. Losing sight of this is what brings about separation and divorce. If you want to get married and stay married, your union should be grounded in what God, Jesus, and the Holy Spirit originally intended marriage to be.

So, what did God originally intend marriage to be? Well, just like everything else in creation, marriage was intended to *physically* reflect God's glory.

> *God created man in his own image, in the image of God he created him; male and female he created them.*
> —Gen. 1:27

There was a visible, divine beauty that reflected off Adam and Eve and was present throughout all creation. If you can imagine, it was heaven on earth. Let's look at the physical events that unfolded before the first-ever coming together of husband and wife.

> And the LORD God planted a garden in Eden . . . and there he put the man [Adam] whom he had formed. And out of the ground the LORD God made to spring up every tree that is pleasant to the sight and good for food.
>
> —Gen. 2:8–9

Imagine walking into your favorite grocery store and all the fruits and vegetables are perfectly ripe, perfectly shaped, and perfect in color. But instead of grabbing them from the produce section, imagine that you're pulling them right out of the garden they grew in and plucking them off their homegrown plants and trees. The Garden of Eden was remarkably filled with the most delicious grapes, the sweetest figs, the crispiest apples, and the most satisfying fruit ever. Adam loved it all so much that he gladly accepted the responsibility of overseeing it.

> The LORD God took the man and put him in the garden of Eden to work it and keep it.
>
> —Gen. 2:15

God Values Marriage Preparation

If you've ever planted a garden, you know it's hard work. Burying the seeds, caring for the soil, and watering day after day requires patience and a commitment to make it grow. Without hesitation, Adam went to work for God. He devoted his time and energy to managing plants and produce. Think about this. Adam was in the middle of paradise with complete individual freedom to do as he wished. Instead of running off on an excursion or a wild adventure, he made the decision to follow God. Instead of choosing to be led by his emotions or his self-identity, Adam chose to be led by objective reality. Allowing himself to be guided by the Holy Spirit and to be of the truth, Adam displayed dedication when the time came to listen to God's voice.

> And the LORD God commanded the man [Adam], saying, "You may surely eat of every tree of the garden, but of the tree of the knowledge of good and evil you shall not eat."
> —Gen. 2:16–17

The fact that Adam didn't run straight to the prohibited tree and eat from it was a clear sign of obedience. His next act proved his allegiance even further by following God's direction and instruction as he named all the animals. This completed task revealed Adam's acceptance of responsibility for everything God gave him. His compliance with the work of God and his participation in the Holy Spirit's ministry was in preparation for the day of Eve's arrival. It was important because while marriage is intended to *physically* reflect God's glory, it is also intended to *spiritually* reflect God's glory. By design, God prepped Adam to love with peace in his heart, to lead with joy in his soul, and to live with discipline in his mind. Those are all characteristics of the Holy Spirit's influence.

> [T]he fruit of the Spirit is love, joy, peace, patience, kindness, goodness, faithfulness, gentleness, self-control.
> —Gal. 5:23

As the Holy Spirit was hovering over the life of Adam, having breathed into his nostrils the breath of life, the man was formed wholesomely and purposed to be an exemplary husband. When the time was right, he was granted a bride. Only when Adam was ready to meet his other half did God put Eve in his life.

> And . . . the LORD God . . . he made . . . a woman and brought her to the man.
>
> —Gen. 2:22

Once Adam and Eve were united with their marriage on full display, the world now had a connection between the spiritual and physical reflection of God's glory. This couple, made in God's image, could experience spiritual love from God but also physical love from each other through intimacy. Together, they could experience spiritual joy in God their Creator but also physical joy through their companionship—watching each other smile, making each other laugh, and pleasing each other with their bodies. This love-producing connection is made possible through the Holy Spirit, and it sets up a marital union through God.

But it was never meant to be broken. Spiritually and physically, the power of love was meant to be ongoing without division, free of pain and difficulty. Here's what that means: God created us to be in constant communion with him, and God created marriage for spouses to have constant communion with each other in him. Total communion with him and in him is the recipe for a phenomenal love life through him.

God Values Full Transparency

The married life that produces the highest joy, the greatest peace, and the purest love is the married life lived completely united to God. But why?

Why does God want to be unified and in community with couples?

Why does he want to be connected to every spouse's thoughts, words, and deeds?

One of the things I coveted before becoming a believer was my privacy—my right to do things alone, on my own, in my own way, and on my own time. That remains a struggle even today, and I've always wondered why. When did my need for personal privacy become such a necessity? And how could I have let myself become so obsessed with it? For the longest time, I had to guard my cell phones with secret passcodes and my laptops with confidential passwords because of the pornographic material that was on them. My sex life had to be sneaky so I didn't get in trouble for doing what I wasn't supposed to be doing. I lied to my family and friends—I lied to myself—to protect my own privacy.

When God created the earth, there was no need for this kind of covering up or isolation. Everything was out in the open, so much so that Adam and Eve could walk around without hiding their bodies.

> And the man [Adam] and his wife [Eve] were both
> naked and were not ashamed.
> —Gen. 2:25

The world God created was filled with perfect freedom. It was visibly good everywhere, shining with complete innocence. There was no need for privacy from God or others. It wasn't until Adam and Eve disobeyed God that they felt shame enough to run and hide, to keep from being exposed.

> [A]nd the man and his wife hid themselves from the
> presence of the LORD God among the trees of the
> garden.
> —Gen. 3:8

I can fully relate to Adam and Eve's response here. When they were running and hiding, avoiding the consequences, trying to right their own wrongs, and freaking out when they got caught, those are all characteristics of my past. Before I became a Christian, I would do things against God's will, opposed to the Spirit's way. In the "world" I created, so to speak, there was addiction and bondage. It was *not* visibly good; it was visibly bad. In *my* world, the guilty got to roam free so I could lie, cheat, and steal. I could deceive. When life began with me and not the Holy Spirit, I could do whatever I wanted. When marriage began with me and not the Holy Spirit, I could do as I pleased. That is why God had to intervene. That is why he had to change my every thought, every word, and every deed.

My story went like this: I was literally destroying myself, poisoning my mind, and hollowing out my heart. God changed all that, not with an invasion of privacy but with his life-giving Spirit. I was deep in the dumps, and the Lord revived my soul. So whatever your story is or whatever your current circumstances are, it's never too late to invite the Holy Spirit into your marriage. He's not there to spy on you or control you. He's there to enlighten you and protect you. Enlightenment happens so you choose light over darkness. But first, he must convict you. Conviction is necessary for you to learn what is righteous. Learning what is righteous helps you choose restoration over ruin. And when you allow the Holy Spirit to educate you and mature you, there is no limit to what he can accomplish for you. He rescues marriages from the worst of problems to bring about the best solutions. His goal is to keep us in the fight for marital unity and to wage war against division, anything that might tear couples apart, even the worst secret sins. God's Word is filled with what we'll need every step of the way. Here's my favorite example:

[W]alk by the Spirit and you will not gratify the desires of the flesh. For the desires of the flesh are against the Spirit, and the desires of the Spirit are against the flesh, for these are opposed to each other, to keep you from doing the things you want to do. . . . [T]hose who belong to Christ Jesus have crucified the flesh with its passions and desires. If we live by the Spirit, let us also keep in step with the Spirit.

—Gal. 5:16–17, 24–25

God bless you on your marriage journey, and may his Spirit equip you with everything you need for battle. I hope that as you continue to turn these pages, you will find each chapter helpful for support.

Chapter 4

Stand against the Schemes

Since the beginning of human history, the institution of marriage has been under attack. Even today, the immense harmony that is supposed to characterize marital union remains at the highest level of threat. It's become common for husbands and wives to tell each other things like "all couples fight" and "every marriage has issues." Those statements are true; however, it's only because of the fallen world we live in. But it wasn't always so. There was a time when divorce wasn't even on the table; a time when separation was unheard of. There was a period in which we had no need for marital counseling or couples therapy and no need for a prenup or alimony. God created a world filled with unending unity and peace. The first husband and wife he made were completely in his image. Adam reflected God's strength and leadership, while Eve equally mirrored God's help and care. Together this couple represented perfect love and dignity.

A slippery snake changed all that. As silly as that sounds, it's true. A treacherous backstabber wormed his way into a position of influence and deceived the very first married couple. His goal was simple: get them to do something God said not to do. When he achieved that, an assault on all future spouses took place. The perfect reflection of God's image in Adam and Eve was shattered, and marriage would never be the same again. Here's how it happened.

> Now the serpent was more crafty than any other beast of the field that the LORD God had made. He said to the woman [Eve], "Did God actually say, 'You shall not eat of any tree in the garden'?" And the woman said to the serpent, "We may eat of the fruit of the trees in the garden, but God said, 'You shall not eat of the fruit of the tree that is in the midst of the garden, neither shall you touch it, lest you die.'" But the serpent said to the woman, "You will not surely die. For God knows that when you eat of it your eyes will be opened, and you will be like God, knowing good and evil." So when the woman saw that the tree was good for food, and that it was a delight to the eyes, and that the tree was to be desired to make one wise, she took of its fruit and ate, and she also gave some to her husband [Adam] who was with her, and he ate.
>
> —Gen. 3:1–6

As you can see, the creation account got a little weird. A talking snake and a mystical tree seem a bit strange. Most people can't see this taking place, but it did. This really happened. And even though some might view this occurrence as highly unlikely, it's still part of our history. Every husband and wife should consider examining the creation narrative and its implications. It helps men and women better comprehend each other. Studying this portion of Scripture can work wonders in your marriage. It reveals much about male and female identity. To understand the root of complications between spouses, we must place the creation narrative under deep scrutiny. So, instead of trying to figure out how a snake could talk, let's take a deeper look at what happened. What we need to see is that for the first time in human history, God's authority and character were being called into question.

We Made a Bad Decision

Never before on earth had there been a creature skeptical of the Creator. Eve, knowing full well who God is and what he said, willfully went against his command. The worst part is that her husband, Adam, who was meant to lead Eve in obedience, literally just stood there and did nothing. He made no attempt to speak up against the serpent's scheme or to prevent his wife from making the gravest mistake of all time—mistrusting God. Rather than taking action, Adam was passive and tolerant. That makes me curious if he thought there was validity to the serpent's claim. His wife sure thought so.

The creation narrative tells us there were four reasons Eve made the decision to eat from the tree. The first was that the fruit looked harmless. Physically it was beautiful to the naked eye. Ladies, it was probably equivalent to your favorite dessert, the one that makes your sweet tooth sing for joy. Guys, imagine it was like a juicy prime tomahawk steak cooked and seasoned to perfection, served sizzling off the grill. Needless to say, it was very tempting. The second reason Eve ate was that she enjoyed looking at it. Once she saw it, she couldn't take her eyes off it. I would imagine that the fruit made her mouth water. Third, Eve thought she and Adam would walk away with more knowledge and more independence. She also believed that their marriage would be better if they broke God's command. As it turned out, that was nowhere near the case. Here's what happened next.

> *Then the eyes of both [Adam and Eve] were opened, and they knew that they were naked. And they sewed fig leaves together and made themselves loincloths. . . . [T]he man and his wife hid themselves from the presence of the LORD God among the trees of the garden. But the LORD God called to the man and said to him, "Where are you?" And he said, "I heard the sound of you in the garden, and I was afraid, because I was naked, and I hid myself." He said, "Who told you that you were naked? Have you eaten of the tree of which I commanded you not to eat?" The man said, "The woman whom you gave to be with me, she gave me fruit of the tree, and I ate." Then the LORD God said to the woman, "What is this that you have done?" The woman said, "The serpent deceived me, and I ate."*
>
> —Gen. 3:7–13

The final reason Eve snatched fruit from the forbidden tree was because she thought an autonomous lifestyle was within her grasp. She thought self-rule and self-law were attainable in this world and that all she had to do was reach for them. Adam and Eve were basically believing a lie, and we see that in their reactions. By eating from the tree, this couple hoped to be held in higher esteem with a boost in confidence and an increase in power. But just the opposite came about. They were filled with insecurity and shame, weakened by fear, wishing they could just crawl under a rock.

I know that feeling all too well, and every time I read their story, I'm reminded of the regret that comes with disobeying God. When I mistreat my wife or lose my patience with her, for example, I remember the mental traps of a slippery snake. If you don't know it already, the serpent in this story is the devil, Satan. He duped Adam and Eve into pursuing autonomy, a quest to be ruled by no one other than themselves. At that moment, the devil performed his first of many pestilent tricks and announced himself as the sworn adversary of God. That means everything God is for, the devil is permanently against.

Satan is opposed to the success of every Christian marriage. His modus operandi is to fill our hearts with lies and deceit, to ruin all chance of fidelity and faithfulness. He wants nothing more than to see all of us at each other's throats, cheating on each other, separated, and divorced. Ever since the marital union between Adam and Eve, the devil has been working to sabotage all efforts for holy matrimony. The worst part, though, is that we've assisted him in the process. You see, the devil can't make us do anything. He can only tempt us with sin. We're the ones who commit sin. Satan merely tempted Eve to disobey God, but it was her decision to actually go through with it. Eve could only share the fruit with Adam, but it was his decision to actually eat it. And the evidence proving they were all at fault was the justice God rendered when they chose wrong over right.

> *The LORD God said to the serpent, "Because you have done this, cursed are you . . . all the days of your life. I will put enmity [Jesus] between you and the woman, and between your offspring and her offspring; he will bruise your head. . . ." To the woman, he said, "I will surely multiply your pain. . . ." And to Adam he said, "Because you have listened to the voice of your wife*

*and have eaten of the tree . . . cursed is the ground
because of you; in pain you shall eat of it all the days
of your life."*

—Gen. 3:14–17

God's command to not eat from the tree was to protect Adam and Eve from negative repercussions. The devil made it appear like God was restricting them. So, God put his foot down and drew a line in the sand. Since then there has been an ongoing fight for good, one in which Jesus sacrificed himself, spilling his blood on the cross for victory over sin and death. But the choice Adam and Eve made for wrong over right, even though it took place thousands of years ago, has definitely left its mark on all of us. You've probably heard the phrase *original sin*. It refers to the consequences of Adam and Eve's disobedience and the effect it has on humanity. When the first married couple acted against God's will, the surety of further defiance became inevitable. Their curse is passing through every generation and continues to spawn a race of people (ourselves included) who will inescapably face chaos and grief. Things like difficulty and death are unavoidable in life. Essentially, original sin makes the human race susceptible to wrongdoing and vulnerable to selfish tendencies. That is why marriages are plagued by pain. It's why spouses yell, argue and break each other's hearts. It's the reason love hurts; it's why husbands and wives cry. It's why there's sometimes anguish in the home.

While it was easy to blame Satan for all this, Adam and Eve should have actually blamed themselves. At any point, they could have just said no. They could have avoided the entire situation had they trusted God and resisted temptation. Sound familiar? It does to me. At times in my life, I have struggled with sobriety, purity, and integrity. Instead of trusting God, I turned to plenty of forbidden fruits. Then I would deal with my mistakes by blaming everyone but myself. However, nobody *made* me do those things. The devil didn't *force* me to do wrong. I did it all on my own. I don't doubt that I was influenced by a toxic culture the devil conjured. But deep down, I did what I wanted to do. The Bible says we all suffer from choosing wrong over right because of original sin.

> *And you were dead in the trespasses and sins in which you once walked, following the course of this world, following the prince of the power of the air, the spirit that is now at work in the sons of disobedience— among whom we all once lived in the passions of our flesh, carrying out the desires of the body and the mind, and were by nature children of wrath, like the rest of mankind.*
>
> —Eph. 2:1–3

The same is true for marital society today. Every day, husbands and wives have a choice. You either follow Jesus and walk by faith or follow the devil and walk in sin. To put it another way, you either walk by the Spirit or gratify the desires of the flesh. We discussed that in previous chapters of this book. Remember, the Holy Spirit is the one who helps us love, honor, and respect our spouses. The flesh, on the other hand, is driven by selfishness and corruption. It is influenced by toxic humanity. Its agenda is to brainwash us so we renounce allegiance to our Creator. Like the devil, it wants us to believe that God's ways are a restriction, not a protection. It wants to trap us, addict us, and then leave us to our own self-destructive devices. God's agenda is much different. For every Christian husband and wife, he has a better plan.

But God, being rich in mercy, because of the great love with which he loved us, even when we were dead in our trespasses, made us alive together with Christ—by grace you have been saved through faith. And this is not your own doing; it is the gift of God.

—Eph. 2:4–8

Formerly, we turned our backs to God, but now we see him for who he really is—our Deliverer. He rescues us from the enemy's attacks and then equips us to fight back. Can you see that in your own life? I see it in mine. In Chapter 3, I told you I got put in handcuffs and hauled off to jail. It was because *externally* I broke the law of the land. But *internally*, I was breaking so much more. Internally, I was breaking the law of God. I was eating from the tree of which he commanded us not to eat. My soul was in the worst terrible condition. The night I was arrested, the police physically confined me to a jail cell, but spiritually, the enemy already had me on lockdown. Satan had snatched me up and trafficked me for dark purposes. He exploited my weaknesses and objectified me as God's enemy in the war on evil.

I was a slave carrying out my natural desires and supporting the devil's creed. To use the Bible's terminology, I was a "son of disobedience." I was stuck in a dark hole that I had dug myself and could not escape unless God intervened. And so he did. The key to setting me free was "the great love with which he loved us." Jesus is the ultimate demonstration of that love. God apprehended me through the sacrifice he made on the cross. My life was so important to him that he held nothing back, not even the life of his own Son. And in nailing my sins to the cross, God took a stand against the schemes of the devil. Why did he do that? He did it because he fights for good. He fights back with love. Another reason is that he had a better plan for my life, and not just for me but for my wife as well. The same is true for you and your spouse. He has better plans for all of us because he knew one day, we would become Christian husbands and wives who need to stick together and fight for each other.

Fight Back with Love

God's plan is to save us from tearing each other apart, to remove the blinders that disable us from being together. He wants to change our dark days into days full of his light. He wants to remove any hate in our hearts and replace it with his love. God knows it is impossible for married couples to be truly fruitful and rightly multiply without the power of his love. He knows that husbands can't lead their wives from a dark hole. He knows a man can't properly love his wife if he's a verbally abusive, porn-addicted "son of disobedience." God also knows that a wife won't be much help to her husband if she's wrapped up in "the passions of the flesh." He knows wives won't truly respect their husbands while they are "children of wrath." For us to see all that, God must bring reconciliation and change. For us to know our spousal roles and have godly marriages, there has to be restoration and ongoing change. If you want a lifelong commitment with your spouse, God must take you from being "dead in our trespasses" to "make you alive" first. Then you can build the strongest foundation for marriage. In living with Jesus, your marriage can thrive off the gift of God—his grace—by which you are saved—through faith. Your faith is what shields you from enemy attacks. Your faith is your first line of defense.

But the first step in fighting back is *love.*

> *Above all, keep loving one another earnestly, since love covers a multitude of sins.*
>
> —1 Pet. 4:8

Together, we fight back and stand against the schemes with love. And it's not just any love; it is God's love. It's not the love we have for money, power, and fame but the love that lays down its life for others. It's not the love we have for food, sports, and entertainment but the love that carries its own cross to a crucifixion. It's love that isn't partial. It's God's, wholehearted love. It's not self-love. It's love that puts others first, a love that endures.

> *Put on then as God's chosen ones, holy and beloved, compassionate hearts, kindness, humility, meekness, and patience, bearing with one another and if one has a complaint against another, forgiving each other; as the Lord has forgiven you, so you also must forgive. And above all these put on love, which binds everything together in perfect harmony.*
>
> —Col. 3:12–14

Once we put on love, we can swallow our pride and stop holding grudges. This might sound cheesy, but when we put on God's love, it's like sending a knockout blow to the enemy's face. The power of God's love is unstoppable in its defense against evil. If you want to protect your marriage, take action with the love of the Lord, and he will back you up.

> *For the eyes of the LORD run to and fro throughout the whole earth, to give strong support to those whose heart is blameless toward him.*
>
> —2 Chron. 16:9

The word *blameless* is one of many Bible words we hardly use anymore. I think it's because all spouses, myself included, have dealt with the pressure of being without blame and have blown it. We've all messed up. We all have flaws in our character, more than we're willing to admit. We all have dark memories and royal screw-ups. The grievous signs of our weaknesses can be very discouraging. When we're discouraged, that's when we tell ourselves, "Nobody's perfect." We freely admit, "We're all sinners." That's true. Those are biblical truths, but we are still the saints of God. As saints, we can rightly pursue blamelessness and holiness, and we should always protect ourselves from tolerating our imperfections and sins. We should never make the decision to function in alliance with our dysfunction. I realize that's easier said than done, especially in marriage. But if Adam and Eve could do it in the midst of a complicated ordeal, with God's love so can we.

Adam and Eve both admitted that what they did was wrong. They both came clean and told God, "I ate." In essence, they admitted their guilt and moved forward. In doing so, they renewed their commitment to their Creator. God graciously forgave Adam and Eve. He cared for them with faithfulness. Out of love and sacrifice, he covered their sins.

> *The LORD God made garments of skins for Adam and his wife and clothed them.*
> —Gen. 3:21 (NIV)

Adam and Eve also renewed their commitment to each other. Despite what transpired, they stayed together and honored God by starting a family.

> *Adam named his wife Eve because she would become the mother of all living. Adam made love to his wife Eve, and she became pregnant and gave birth to Cain. She said, "With the help of the LORD I have brought forth a man." Later she gave birth to his brother Abel.*
> —Gen. 3:20, 4:1–2 (NIV)

This is great news for us. If Adam and Eve had split up and decided to be alone, none of us would have ever been born. If God had not loved them and given them grace, none of us would have had a chance at life. I hope you realize it is love that makes the world go 'round. Do you see that? Here's what I see. Adam and Eve were both in a pinch, and their marriage was suffering. They were in a state of panic, pain, and separation. They were pointing fingers and assigning blame. They were desperate to get bailed out of their embarrassing situation. I can almost hear them praying what I used to pray when my disobedience got me in trouble— "Oh, please God, if you could just get me out of this mess, I promise, I won't do it again."

That is how I used to treat God. I would go to him only when I needed help. I would consult him only when I was desperate. Each time I was in a bind, I would pray, "God, can you fix this and make it like it never happened so I can return to my normal life?" That is what Adam and Eve wanted, a chance to go back to the way things were. But it was too late, and things would never be the same again. They learned the hard way that their decisions had real meaning and therefore real consequences. It was love that pulled them through to recovery.

Think back on your own marriage. Have you ever had to learn anything the hard way and suffer the consequences? If you have, then you know that giving in to the schemes of the devil causes hurt and pain. When we give in to our temptations, it does violence to our souls. If you've ever hidden things from your spouse or lied to them about something, you've seen the brokenness that occurs and the assault that takes place in a marriage relationship. There were some dark seasons along my Christian walk that tested my faith, and I questioned my allegiance to God. There were times when I wasn't standing against the schemes but participating in them and playing the victim card with God every time I got caught. The scheme I fell for the most was sexual pleasure and its false promise to keep me satisfied. My forbidden fruit was premarital sex, and it had been since I was a teenager. Premarital sex was also a struggle for me as an adult.

After I became a Christian, purity was a struggle. For the most part, being single was a lonely journey for me. I dealt with it by giving in to lust, which revealed a lack of self-control in my heart. I used to think that once I got married, I'd be free from the struggle to stay pure. But as most spouses know, after you get married, the lust stays with you. At least it did for me after I married Brittany. Because of my previous experience with sex, I would draw comparisons to her. You can imagine how she must have felt when all this junk surfaced. It was awful. I was never tempted with an affair—thank God—but you can be sure my wife felt uneasy enough. Newlyweds typically go through a romantic honeymoon phase. Not us. We went through a nightmare phase. Do you know why? Because I didn't take a stand against the schemes.

Brittany and I spent the first year of our marriage dealing with the complications of my past. Heated conversations were the norm, and we could never keep a consistent mood. Each time we fought, the enemy gained a foothold and created distance between us. It was a struggle to follow Jesus and walk by faith. Giving in to sin is always the easier route, but you can never control the mess you leave behind. And it got messy. Brittany and I needed to have that come-to-Jesus moment regarding my royal screw-ups and her tiny mistakes. Both of us were responsible for our marriage—not just me and not just her. When we came to realize that, we owned up to what we had done wrong, and God helped us to do right *together*. Love is what pulled us through to recovery.

Whenever the enemy is given a foothold, it causes a division between you and your spouse. The enemy's job is to shame you and guilt trip you so you will run and hide from each other. The enemy knows that the stress of isolating yourselves will make you bitter and that pulling away from each other will depress you. Once you're bitter and depressed, the guilt and shame will make you avoid friends and family members, which poisons your joy. It all takes its toll, and it's all part of the enemy's plan so spouses will be miserable. That is why it's so important to be immersed in the love of God. Love leads us to honesty. Honesty guides us to the confession of sin. Confession brings us out of our misery and into the light. Where there is light, there is truth. The truth also fights our battles.

> *If we confess our sins, [God] is faithful and just to forgive us our sins and to cleanse us from all unrighteousness.*
>
> —1 John 1:9

Tear Down the Walls

When you rely on God to *cleanse* you, he is *faithful and just* to make your marriage right. He sends his Holy Spirit to give you strong support. Why? Because standing against the schemes of the devil doesn't come naturally to us. Doing the right thing is an uphill climb. It's a struggle that seems to have no end. The straight and narrow path is a hike, not a cakewalk. Some days you'll want to quit, and some nights you'll wonder if the cost of following Jesus is really worth it. There will be times when you tell yourself, "I can't do this anymore." I know because I've told myself that. But it's not our moral success that makes us clean; it's God's forgiveness. And it's Jesus who makes us blameless (John 14:6). So whenever you feel like giving up, tell yourself the last thing Jesus said to us before he died on the cross— "It is finished" (John 19:30). The work has been done! Believe that Jesus has overcome all our weaknesses.

Remember when I mentioned that the heavy burden of guilt and fear was like carrying around a backpack full of bricks? Well, when I married Brittany, I never got rid of that backpack full of bricks. I brought it with me into my marriage. Whenever Brittany and I had a conflict, those bricks would come out and stack up between us. Each brick represented a foothold for the enemy, something problematic. Those bricks were things like resentment toward her for disagreeing with me; things like pointing fingers, assigning blame or throwing our past mistakes in each other's faces. Another example was her not wanting to have sex or be intimate with me. I used to think my lust was her fault. I criticized *her* when lust got the best of me. If she was disrespectful, I'd lay more bricks down between us. If she was insecure and ultrasensitive—more bricks. If she made accusations—more bricks. Before long, there was a wall of separation that gave her no hope for change. She'll even tell you that talking to me was like talking to a brick wall. The higher she climbed up it to work things out, the more bricks I piled on. You see, the enemy's foothold is nothing more than a barrier comprised of your bad habits. It's an obstruction to unity and peace.

Every day that barrier stood between us. Brittany and I were in despair. We were falling apart. But it turned out to be a necessary roadblock because we were headed down a path playing right into the devil's schemes. We just didn't see it at first. What we discovered together was that marriage doesn't thrive on who's right or wrong; it thrives on forgiveness and grace. We discovered we'd never be able to decide what was best for our marriage on our own. But we knew God was able. He was able then, and he is able now. While Brittany and I spiraled out of control, we weren't growing in love, and we almost lost each other. What we remembered was that marriage is about God. We didn't get married to meet each other's needs; we got married in honor of him who has met our greatest need. So, we humbled ourselves, and forgiveness poured in. After that, Brittany and I took a sledgehammer to that brick wall. Brick by brick we tore it down into pieces. We got rid of the animosity and put an end to our marital feud.

Yes, we still have issues. We still argue sometimes. Our marriage isn't perfect, and it's never going to be. But that doesn't mean we can't fight for perfection with the blameless love of God. Yes, we'll still mess up. We're still sinners. But the difference now is that we'll remind each other of whose side we're on. Instead of fighting each other, we'll fight for the goodness of God in our marriage. We will fight for lifelong love and marriage that lasts. I hope the same for you. I pray that all husbands and wives fight for the goodness of God to unite them. It is our spiritual duty to protect our marriages from attacks and guard against the assault on our spouses. When we stand against the schemes of the snake and learn from our mistakes, God equips us to combat the enemy's battlefront. In doing so, the world sees firsthand the testimony of God's love winning. It sees him victorious over brokenness and shame.

Chapter 5

Strengthen Your Faith for Marriage

I didn't struggle with cold feet at the altar when I married Brittany. I had fallen head over heels in love with her. There was no doubt in my mind that she was the one for me. Brittany and I knew that God had brought us together. We knew he had a plan to make us husband and wife. Getting married helped us further define our love for each other and our love for God. But in the beginning, I wondered if maybe we should have waited, not because I was unsure about spending the rest of my life with her but because I still had some growing up to do. I was still somewhat immature. I was happy to become a husband, but all my bad habits weren't just going to magically disappear. Marriage wasn't necessarily the remedy for my disingenuous lifestyle. In my case, having a spouse revealed some underlying issues in my heart. Brittany will tell you she also wasn't exactly in the best place spiritually. It was hard to let go of our troubled pasts. We were struggling with things such as shame and guilt, bitterness and anger, insecurity and lust.

We both had faith, but it had been weakened by our circumstances. We both were Christians, but we weren't fully following Jesus. We needed to get right with God. For too long, our beliefs hadn't been accompanied by many good works, and that bothered us. Fellowship was lacking, our prayer time was slim, and we weren't studying the Bible enough. Those things are supposed to characterize the life lived on a mission for God, especially for us because ministry is a huge passion for us. But while we were in that funk, we sort of put Jesus on the back burner. Thankfully, it wasn't for long. We had talked about plugging deeper into the church and participating in more outreach. We wanted to help people and volunteer our time and our resources. All those things we wanted to do together, side by side. We were ready to go for it. So we got right with God and then got hitched.

Looking back, I thought tying the knot might make life easier for us. It seemed like a step in the right direction for a couple that got off track. But early on, our marriage took a turn for the worse. We were desperate for help. Our foundation was fragile and built mostly on emotion. We needed something firm to build on, something solid, not shaky. That *something* needed to be the source of our convictions, our reason for being together in the first place. No doubt about it—it had to be the Lord. There is no other perfect source to stand firm on besides God. He is everything that gives us marital hope and marital peace. Through him, we have an identity in Jesus who is the cornerstone for success being husband and wife. From him flows every good desire inside of us.

I have found that if step one in fighting the attacks on marriage is to *love,* then step two is to *strengthen your faith.*

[B]e strong in the LORD *and in the strength of his might. Put on the whole armor of God, that you may be able to stand against the schemes of the devil.*

—Eph. 6:10–11

What this verse means is that you cannot function effectively on weak faith. Without strong faith, you are in danger of being consumed by the schemes of the enemy. You and your spouse can fall under attack at any time. Without armor, you won't be able to withstand the enemy clobbering through your marriage. Think about it like this: Before soldiers go into battle, they must undergo rigorous training and conditioning. After they're shaped up, they're given a Kevlar, flak jacket, camouflage, night vision, fire-retardant gloves, pads, and all kinds of tactical gear. Soldiers need to be fully protected from injury because, during an all-out war, their enemy is out to destroy them. They must make wise decisions to survive and protect themselves from death. Soldiers also educate themselves on all types of warfare so they don't get captured and taken prisoner. The enemy's torment can make a soldier's life very painful. So they must equip their minds to be sharp. They train their bodies physically to be tough and strong. The same applies spiritually to all Christian husbands and wives.

Every morning you wake up, there is a war going on, and your soul is a prime target. Every day that you have breath in your lungs and blood pumping through your veins, there is a battle taking place between good and evil. Everywhere you go is a battleground. Your mission is this: in everything you do, fight for what's right, and resist temptation into enemy territory. You must never drop bombs for wrongdoing's sake. Through every conflict, you must keep in mind whose side you're on. Remember that deep within every born again Christian is an *old self* fiercely trying to unleash its ulterior motives. The *new self* is devoted to the mission of God (pure motives), while the old self is obsessed with power and control. The old self ambushes the new self every chance it gets. In its pride, it must have the final word; it must always be right so it can come out on top. Having the readiness to protect your new self, strengthens you to counterstrike your old self.

Don't Be Unprepared

Whatever you're going through in your marriage, if you're like me, you know sharing life with a spouse is tough. It's an adjustment that can seem overwhelming at times. Before I married Brittany, I'd been divorced for 14 years. Over that period, I'd grown as a Christian man. I'd gained wisdom. But I was nowhere near ready to be the best husband I could be. I had dated a bunch of women, but practice doesn't necessarily make perfect in that arena. And it's not practicing if you're just playing games, which I was. Those women were at a disadvantage because I was secretly looking for someone to take care of me instead of me taking care of them. That's probably why none of them took me seriously when it came to discussing marriage. It's no wonder I got dumped a lot. I was struggling with my old, selfish ways.

I'll admit that dating was most often a way for me to deal with my loneliness. Sadly, it was like a hobby, an extracurricular activity. When I look at my past, I don't see a guy preparing to be a husband. I see a guy pursuing women to make his life as comfortable and convenient as possible. I see a guy oblivious to women's needs and self-absorbed by his own needs. I spent over a decade as a single divorcé growing accustomed to my private lifestyle instead of creating space for a lifelong companion. My two oldest sons visited me every summer, but aside from that, I lived on my own. I had my own room and my space. I liked being able to come and go as I pleased. I didn't have to make my bed in the morning. I could leave the toilet seat up, pile dishes in the sink, and let the garbage sit. I could have guys' night every night and do whatever I wanted and get away with it. I never had to share anything.

That's not the case anymore. I'm married to Brittany, and now that I'm her husband, I share all kinds of responsibilities. If I leave dishes in the sink, Brittany calls me out on it. If I tried to have a guy's night every night, she'd "kill" me (not literally, of course). I can't be married and come and go as I please—that doesn't honor my wife. I can't leave the house a mess—that puts an extra burden on her. I have to set an example now for Brittany and lead by that example. I can't afford to be lazy. I can't just look out for myself anymore. My wife and I are one. We're united. My bathroom and bedroom are now also *her* bathroom and bedroom. It's now *our* closet. It's *our* kitchen. It's *our* bank account. Everything that's mine is also hers. I surely wasn't ready for all that.

When I was single, I wasn't preparing to share everything I owned. Instead, I focused on having all things to myself. I wasn't looking for a soulmate; I was looking for someone to make me feel good. I was searching for significance and someone to stroke my ego. I have to confess that at the beginning of my relationship with Brittany, that's what I was doing with her. I was using her. She was vulnerable, and I took advantage of that. Ladies, does that sound like a guy you'd want to spend the rest of your life with? Does it sound like I had a clue as to what marriage was? Heck no. It's a good thing Brittany saw past all that. She saw a man who was capable of much more. She saw a guy who was selling himself short of God's blessings for the empty promises of the world. I was a wannabe ladies' man who had unprioritized his call to be a true follower of Jesus.

I am so thankful Brittany came into my life. We were the best of friends while we were dating. We had some rough times back then, but still, her wisdom was a positive influence on me. Her genuine sincerity served as a combatant to my ongoing foolery. She was never afraid to call me out or check my behavior. Even though we were both struggling in our walks, she inspired me to be a good Christian. She reminded me of how men are supposed to conduct themselves. Her positive influence energized me. She made me want to put on the whole armor of God at a time when I was more interested in taking it off. I had never been challenged by past girlfriends the way Brittany challenged me. She motivated me to be a better man, father, brother, and son. I loved that about her.

Brittany was unlike any woman I had ever spent time with. That was good but also hard for me. It was good because God placed her in my life at the right moment, but it was hard because she needed to talk through every single dispute. Communication was never my strong suit. I hated talking through things. I avoided it like the plague. Confrontation is hard, awkward, and almost always inconvenient. But communication and confrontation are important to Brittany. Every conflict, every argument, every disagreement—she needed everything resolved with clarity. In the past, I would get into an argument with a woman, and we'd just sleep on it; we didn't have to talk about our problems. We'd just get over it, say sorry, and make up. Or we'd sweep it under the rug and pretend like it never happened. If there was ever a major fight while I was dating, I'd just withdraw. If the relationship got too tough, I'd use the silent treatment. That was my solution to everything. But I found that the silent treatment is a characteristic of the old self. Whenever I used it in my marriage, it always made things worse.

Take Responsibility

Have you ever used the silent treatment? Did it fill you with pride and make you bitter toward your spouse? The silent treatment is an escape from the responsibility of seeking forgiveness. It's manipulative, and it's a poor attempt at justifying separation. I believe the most crucial time to be with your spouse is when you want nothing more than to be apart from them. That was one of the hardest things for me to learn. It was so hard that Brittany and I had to see a marriage counselor.

The frequent fights and blowups were convincing us more and more that neither of us was getting through to the other. Brittany was seeing things in me that I didn't think were there, and I'd been correcting her in ways she didn't feel she needed to be corrected. I anticipated getting marriage counseling but for the wrong reasons. I viewed it as my chance to be proved right so Brittany could finally apologize. I couldn't wait for her to be told by a third party that she was the one who needed to change. As I write this sentence, I can't help but shake my head because during our first counseling session, I discovered I was so wrong.

Everything—I mean everything—was my fault. That's how I felt. Sitting in that first session across from our male marriage counselor was a colossal facepalm moment. I was so frustrated because he was a guy, too, a man just like me. I was expecting support in accordance with the guy code. I thought to myself, *Dude, whose side are you on?* I blew off his evaluation even though he was right on. He had me figured out. Of course, I got mad. I wasn't mature enough to listen to what he had to say, and, I couldn't help but feel like Brittany was getting away with "her stuff." Mostly I was mad because I felt our marriage counselor focused too much on me. But his approach was completely biblical, and his assessment was spot on. He could see right through me. Still, I thought, *What about her stuff, her disrespect, and her insecurity?* How was I just supposed to overlook all that? I couldn't. The whole thing was embarrassing to me. I felt exposed, so I wanted her to feel exposed. I felt inadequate, so I wanted her to feel inadequate. I wanted to shame her. Deep down I didn't want what was best for our marriage, I wanted Brittany to learn her lesson. I thought that if I could just reveal her incompetence, it might restore the appearance of my competence. I'll stop right there and ask you this question: Do you know what happened then?

My old self had set up an ambush on my new self. Remember, the old self is obsessed with power and control. And here's why: Our old self wants nothing more than to play god. That's the reason it has to have the final word (as God ultimately does). That's why it wants to come out on top (as God ultimately does). I was trying to play god. I couldn't get control of the situation, and it bothered me something fierce. I felt I was being treated unfairly, and forced to take the blame for something I didn't do. That wasn't the case, but because I was hungry for retaliation, my old self started feeding me lies. Those lies in turn produced bitterness and resentment. But then the Holy Spirit helped me. My new self was spiritually dehydrated, so the Holy Spirit had me drink the truth. His remedy was the living water of the Word of God. Listen to this beautiful truth that strengthened me and guided me away from the dangerous mistake of playing god.

> [W]hile we were still weak, at the right time Christ died for the ungodly. . . . God shows his love for us in that while we were still sinners, Christ died for us. . . . For if while we were enemies we were reconciled to God by the death of his Son, much more, now that we are reconciled, shall we be saved by his life. More than that, we also rejoice in God through our Lord Jesus Christ, through whom we have now received reconciliation.
>
> —Rom. 5:6, 8, 10–11

These verses reminded me of how I turned my back on God. All testimonies of saving faith, including yours and mine, begin with our backs turned to God. So, reconciliation was initiated with Jesus dying for us. In every believer's story, God gently turns them around so they can see him face to face—not to be accused, not be blamed or judged, but to be face to face with grace. Every sinner is reconciled with grace, and it starts with Jesus forgiving their weaknesses and wrongdoings. We were once his enemies, but now we are his friends. And we are sealed with God's Spirit, a spirit of peace, poured out on the ungodly to end the war. Those verses remind me of how the battle was won with sacrificial love.

Now, back to my marriage. You see, my wife didn't need me to teach her a lesson; she needed gentleness and kindness from her husband. She didn't need a judge and jury; she needed grace. She needed her companion—me. I wasn't fully there for her. It's because I was too concerned with being there for myself. I was so focused on myself that I neglected her. Once I realized that, I felt remorse. I felt like a microbe like I'd been hit by a Mack truck. I knew our struggle was my fault. No matter what Brittany had said or done, I knew I was failing her as a husband. I was being careless. The yelling, the screaming, and the isolation got me nowhere with my wife. It was wasted time—time I could have spent strengthening my faith for marriage, time I could have spent caring for Brittany, building her up, and edifying her. Instead, I was backing her into a corner and guilt-tripping her to openly admit her shortcomings.

My wife and I were under attack, and instead of manning up with the strength of God, I folded under the pressure. Instead of gearing up for the assault with the whole armor of God, I gave the order to retreat. I let my marriage be invaded by an army of darkness, and as a result, my wife was hurt. Our home was raided by the frontlines of the enemy, and like Adam, I stood by and watched. I couldn't guard the marital watchtower to protect my bride, and like Eve, I let mayhem storm in. I had forgotten what the Word says about the things we can't see that are out to get us.

For we do not wrestle against flesh and blood, but against the rulers, against the authorities, against the cosmic powers over this present darkness, against the spiritual forces of evil in the heavenly places.

—Eph. 6:12

It wasn't my flesh-and-blood spouse I was up against; it was the spiritual forces of evil. Part of what that verse means is that because of powers over the world's present darkness, the battle inside the mind can be more real than the physical battle of the body. For example, spousal mistreatment doesn't start with a physical altercation between a husband and wife. It starts with a mind that craves superiority instigated by dark rulers and authorities within the enemy's ranks. Instead of thinking about how to overcome that craving, the mind succumbs to it. Then once the mind is convinced to lash out, the heart takes action to inflict pain to get its way. If you and your spouse are having overheated arguments, there might be some spiritual forces of evil gunning for you. If you've had blowups, that could be the result of suppressed, deep-seated, evil desire. Evil desire lurks before it becomes obvious. It reveals itself in many forms such as uncontrollable rage or spousal dominance, as well as money-grubbing greed or obsession with extramarital fantasies. Those are just a few examples that characterize couples on the brink of divorce.

Avoid Pitfalls

When forces of evil mess with a marriage, it digs a pit filled with spiritual darkness. Spiritual darkness is the most dangerous place for spouses to linger. It's also the worst time for couples to be stagnant in faith. I know because I've been there. Spiritual darkness existed in every single one of my relationships. That includes my first marriage (as a nonbeliever) and the start of my marriage to Brittany (as a believer). There are two types of pits that spiritual darkness can create.

The first pit—I call it "the nonbeliever pit"—is impossible to get out of because you don't realize you're in it. As we discussed in Chapter 4, it is the pit where one is "dead in the trespasses and sins in which they once walked," following the spiritual darkness trail. When I was in the nonbeliever pit, it was kind of like being a zombie. Everyone I came in contact with suffered in some way, shape, or form. I was out of control, functioning from a self-centered place of ignorance. All I cared about was myself. All I wanted was to benefit m*yself* by satisfying my wants and catering to my needs. It didn't matter who got hurt in the process. The nonbeliever pit is nothing more than a pit of despair. Everyone in it is without hope and God. They're like zombies infected with the virus of ill will and sickening apathy. When you're living like a zombie on the road to nowhere, there is only one outcome. It's called destruction. And the only cure is the grace of God through faith in Christ. Believing in Jesus is the only way to get set free from the pit of the walking dead. Only Jesus can heal the hopeless and bring a new outcome. That's called the plan of salvation.

> *For God did not send his Son into the world to condemn the world, but in order that the world might be saved through him.*
>
> —John 3:17

That's what happened to me. As I was digging my own grave farther into spiritual darkness, God sent Jesus into my life, not to condemn me but to reach his mighty arm and strong hand into the pit to rescue me. There was great healing that day. Being born again empowered me to learn the correct view of marriage. It taught me how God views women, how Jesus treated women, and how the Holy Spirit guides men to properly engage with the opposite sex. So, if you are a Christian, you've been empowered as well. God hasn't condemned you; he's rescued you! He has mended your brokenness and brought light to your darkness. And for your marriage, he provides you with the strength to keep that famous wedding vow, "'til death do us part." He positions all believing spouses in his grace so we can love and care for each other. These things don't come naturally. The Lord gives them to us through his Word and then instructs us on virtues such as dignity and respect.

But sometimes we forget. Sometimes we let those virtues slip our minds. I sure did. And that's how I fell into the second pit—the believer pit. I call it the believer pit because it's a pit of despair, but it has access to hope. As Christians, we struggle with right and wrong, but the difference is that we have the law of God to know right from wrong. On the other hand, nonbelievers are more concerned with the law of the land than the law of God. They don't define right and wrong by God's standards but by their own. For example, as a nonbelieving husband in my first marriage, I often got stinking drunk, but never once did I think that was evil. I probably knew drunkenness wasn't good for me, but I never thought it separated me from God. I was more aware of how it could separate me from society—such as land me in jail or prison. I was more worried about what could get me fired from work—such as showing up under the influence. But I never thought that made a difference on where my soul would end up—heaven versus hell.

In the believer pit, God's grace gives his people ears to hear and eyes to see. When we get stuck in the muck, God reminds believers of their faith. The Holy Spirit also gets down in the trenches. He speaks the truth to those who need it. When I fell into the believer pit, he spoke to me. He brought to my attention the things I did wrong and showed me how I hurt my marriage. But he also reminded me that I wasn't without hope. All I had to do was look up to see the light, to see Jesus. Christian husbands trapped in the believer pit have Jesus as their strength. That strength is what brought me to repentance. With the help of the Holy Spirit, I climbed out of the pit. But in order to stop hurting my marriage, I had to remember what the Scripture says about caring for my wife. Here are a few reminders that helped me.

> *Husbands, love your wives, and do not be harsh with them.*
>
> —Col. 3:19

> *Husbands should love their wives as their own bodies. He who loves his wife loves himself.*
>
> —Eph. 5:28

> *Husbands live with your wives in an understanding way, showing honor to the woman.*
>
> —1 Pet. 3:7

God's Word Provides Transforming Strength

As a Christian husband, I am commanded to live in the light, not in a pit. I am freed to be a light to the rest of the world. All Christian spouses share that responsibility. The Bible makes this very clear. God's people are to shine holistically with love and grace in good and bad, through thick and thin, in weakness and strength. My faith cannot afford to be oppressed by darkness, and neither can my wife's. Brittany and I weren't going to live our lives in a pit, so we cried out to God for rescue. Here are a couple of verses that helped us get our marriage back to a position of strength.

Do all things without grumbling or disputing, that you may be blameless and innocent, children of God without blemish in the midst of a crooked and twisted generation, among whom you shine as lights to the world, holding fast to the word of life.

—Phil. 2:14–16

[S]o as to walk in a manner worthy of the Lord, fully pleasing to him: bearing fruit in every good work and increasing in the knowledge of God; being strengthened with all power, according to his glorious might, for all endurance and patience with joy; giving thanks to the Father, who has qualified you to share in the inheritance of the saints in light. He has delivered us from the domain of darkness and transferred us to the kingdom of his beloved Son, in whom we have redemption, the forgiveness of sins.

—Col. 1:10–14

I hope when you read those verses, they blow your mind as they did mine. They're filled with so much depth that when I read them, I'm utterly undone. It's as if God is announcing to me that apart from him, I can't do anything for my marriage. That's what I hear the Holy Spirit speak to me, and he's right. Without God, we spouses are lost. Without being transferred from the domain of darkness to the kingdom of his beloved Son, we can't have eyes to fully see what marriage is about. In the darkness, marriage is typically minimized to a cultural romantic tradition. It's just a contractual agreement between two parties, a license to sleep together and make legitimate babies. In the darkness, marriage is typically sexualized and materialized. But in the light, marriage is so much more! In the light, it's a unifying, purposeful means of bringing God glory. In the light, marriage is about submitting to God's will. It's about experiencing true contentment through the strength and power of Jesus's love. Those verses changed my outlook as a husband. I rarely thought about what was fully pleasing to God because I was busy living life for myself.

Let's be honest here.

Are we even aware that as Christian husbands and wives our marriages are to reflect conduct in a manner worthy of the Lord? I sure wasn't. What I was doing was living in a manner worthy of myself. I never wanted to do all things without complaining.

And how could I possibly live my life fully pleasing to him?

How could I be blameless? The answer is I can't. None of us can without redemption—the forgiveness of sins.

When we are redeemed, Jesus becomes our blamelessness, and by his power, we are strengthened to follow him. But the battle will continue, which is why we must have endurance and patience with joy. There is a dark domain that is against God's idea of marriage. It is comprised of a crooked and twisted generation that wants to distort purity and pervert faithfulness. It appeals to our wants and inches us toward things such as pornography and adultery. It is given to things like foul language and spousal abuse. It wants to remove God from the picture. It wants us to be sensual and mislead us to think that being promiscuous is acceptable. So we must be strengthened. We must hold fast to the word of life and increase our knowledge of God.

The crooked and twisted generation doesn't want us to strengthen our faith; they want us to give in and join them. They don't want us to shine as lights to the world; they want us to blend in with the darkness. And we can relate. Remember, we were all once part of the dark domain. We formerly relished in sin and dabbled in darkness. We once went rogue and off the deep end. Before we became Christians, we were crooked and twisted, but not anymore. Now we belong to the generation of life and love, the generation that strives for peace and unity, the generation that relishes in the liberty and freedom of Jesus. Now we fight the good fight. Now we live for something bigger than ourselves, greater than anything we've ever known or will know.

If we are strong in the Lord, we'll be able to see marriage through to the end. With God's strength, anything this world throws at us will eventually be overcome. With Jesus's strength, marriage can last. And through the help of the Holy Spirit, love can endure. That makes my heart glad, and I hope it overwhelms your heart with happiness. Happiness, which we'll discuss in the next chapter, is an important strength for all marriages.

Chapter 6

Happy Spouse, Happy House

I spent the better part of my life trying to figure out what makes me happy. When I was single, it was drinks, women, and sex. Those were my top three, followed by entertainment, exotic food, and sports. During that season of life, I was confusing worldly pleasure with genuine happiness. That's why for the longest time I had no filter for what I chased after. It was crazy the amount of money I spent and the things I did to make myself happy. As a bachelor, I deviated from moral standards to stay "happy." Sometimes I even compromised principles to get my way. I ignored guidelines that could have kept my eyes from smut and my ears from obscenities. "Anything goes" was pretty much my motto unless I was around people who might judge me for it. Then and only then was I on my best behavior. Sounds hypocritical, doesn't it?

Having to be one way in secret and another way in the open was easy for me at first. But it wasn't long before the things that made me happy became my obsession. During those obsessive years, I was irritated that I had to live a double life. That irritation resulted in terrible mood swings that slowly produced a bitterness that I was unable to hide. When everything surfaced as it always does, my lies were exposed, and a lot of people got hurt. No one could trust me anymore. Nobody knew who I really was. The saddest part was that I didn't know who I really was. I couldn't recognize my face in the mirror anymore. That is where pleasure-seeking took me—to the middle of an identity crisis.

What Is Happiness?

The pursuit of happiness can teach a person how to love, how to care, and how to experience success. But if done incorrectly, it could make them lie, cheat, and steal. The pursuit of happiness can be characterized by nobility or neglect. It can be attributed to self-preservation or self-sabotage. In marriage, pursuing happiness can be a couple's dream come true or their worst nightmare. It can be a source of marital prosperity, or it can backfire into domestic oblivion. Perhaps you know what I'm talking about. If you're anything like me, you've seen the negative effects of incessantly catering to your own needs. Maybe you were once in the rut I was in. Or maybe you're there now. Either way, during that difficult lapse, an important question I had to ask myself was, "Do I even know what happiness is?"

That question led to more questions. Where did I get my definition of happiness? Was I born with it? Where did I learn how to be happy? Isn't happiness supposed to be constant? Why does it come and go? Those questions gave a whole new meaning to a song I learned when I was little. You know the one. We sang it in kindergarten. It taught us that if you're happy and you know it, clap your hands, stomp your feet, and shout "Hooray!" If you're happy and you know it, then your face will surely show it. I think I always participated in that song. Does that mean happiness is just an emotion?

Here's a quick glimpse into what my youth was like. When I look back on my childhood, I consider it to be a happy one overall. Sure, there were times when things didn't go my way. There were times when I cried and felt pain. I suffered some cuts and bruises. I broke a collarbone and gashed my skin a time or two. I was lucky enough to undergo only one painful surgery. So, for the most part, my childhood was pretty good. I can recall a few fights and arguments with a handful of other kids and a few heated conversations with some young knuckleheads. My parents were strict, and so were my teachers and principals. I was disciplined a lot, but overall, I can't complain.

I remember my family not having a lot of money, but that never bothered me. My folks did the best they could with what they had, and that's all my siblings and I could hope for. My dad wasn't a rich man, but he and my mom kept a roof over our heads. Our house was tiny, but from what I remember, we were always provided for. We were middle-class people residing in a small town in South Texas. We were simple-minded and Catholic. We went to church almost every Sunday and catechism during the week. At home, we were taught manners, politeness, and proper etiquette. Mom and Dad challenged us to get straight A's in school and taught us to work hard. They wanted us to learn to avoid financial struggle and societal difficulty. I was raised to not procrastinate and not be idle. The way I was brought up felt like a recipe for avoiding poverty, being debt-free, and not being poor. My parents taught me to pull my weight and earn success. My dad always told me, "If you fail to plan, you plan to fail." He didn't want me to waste my life or become a screw-up. There were moments when I thought he was too hard on me.

By the time I started junior high, I knew I was unhappy. I wanted to do my own thing and go my own way. I liked goofing off. I liked being rebellious and not taking anything seriously. I continued that pattern of behavior all through high school. My senior year was when I met my now ex-wife. That's around when she got pregnant with Michael, my firstborn. I had already enlisted in the military and was set to ship out after graduation. With the level of responsibility I was suddenly taking on, you'd think that a light bulb would turn on in my head or I would get a wake-up call. Nope. I kept going my own way and doing my own thing. I had my own idea of what life was supposed to be like, and I wasn't going to make changes for anyone. I was living out *my* definition of happiness. When I became an adult and moved out of my parent's house, I had the same attitude of doing things my way. Even though Michael's birth taught me to love unconditionally, my definition of happiness remained self-focused at its core. Even though being in the Marines matured me, the world still revolved around my satisfaction. By the time I was married to my first wife, I had become a miserable man-child. Here's why:

Happiness doesn't begin with what makes *me* happy; it begins with what makes God happy. My heart can never decide what true happiness is, but God can—in this life and the next, now and forever. While I was spiraling out of control on a path of selfish hedonism, I was all smiling on the outside, but there was darkness and gloom on the inside. Living my own way and doing my own thing sucked the life out of me. It was pointless. Trying to make myself happy was a futile pursuit for one reason and one reason only: *God is the giver of joy.* According to Scripture, happiness comes as we put our Maker first and foremost.

Delight yourself in the LORD, and he will give you the desires of your heart.
—Ps. 37:4

Taste and see that the LORD is good. How happy is the person who takes refuge in him!
—Ps. 34:8

True Happiness Originates from God

Our Creator is the main source of happiness. He is the author of pure and unadulterated satisfaction. We can never be completely happy without him. There will never be anything more satisfying than having a relationship with God. Knowing him and being fathered by him bring a level of happiness to our hearts that none could ever think possible in this life. Nothing compares to the joy and peace God has to offer. His gifts and blessings are unparalleled. This is where a lot of people disagree with me because secular society doesn't accept the fact that true happiness flows from the heart of God. Not many in our culture are brought up to believe that. They're not taught it in public schools, community colleges, or universities. They rarely hear about God's love on TV or radio because it's not what sells. What sells is celebrity life, fortune, fame, and sex. That is what the media projects as meaningful happiness. The gospel of Jesus Christ is far from being mainstream. Most non-Christians claim God's Word is outdated and irrelevant and brush it off as fake news.

Many say that the idea of God is pathetic and that following Jesus inevitably leads to unhappiness. They believe that religion is actually to blame for the world's divisiveness. They debate against having a biblical perspective and see no advantage to faith in Christ. They'd rather pretend God doesn't exist and imagine there's no heaven or hell. "Do whatever makes you happy," they say. For them, happiness is found by living in the moment. If there's anyone who knows that's a complete myth, it's yours truly. I've tried everything under the sun to make myself happy. Nothing the world has to offer can ultimately satisfy—not money, not fame. Nothing on earth comes close to the ultimate happiness God bestows on his people. That's been true since the early days of creation. It has been that way since the beginning of time.

> *God saw everything that he had made, and behold, it was very good.*
> —Gen. 1:31

That phrase *very good* is all-encompassing. Seeing everything God made is our starting point for human happiness. Beholding that it was very good is our reference point to the definition of human happiness. Once creation was complete, once man and woman were joined together, God provided happiness in its most pristine form. When Adam and Eve were unified, there was no such thing as marital stress. There was only marital bliss. Before the fall, the sun rose each day and set each night—life only got happier. As Adam and Eve deepened their marital intimacy, happiness in its most pristine form increased and abounded. All this was the direct result of everything God made and it is very good. That might be difficult to understand because, unlike Adam and Eve, we've never experienced happiness in a sinless, peaceful state. Unlike Adam and Eve, we all were brought into the world after the fall. We only know happiness as the absence of misery and sadness. Scripture is clear that our meaning of happiness comes from God.

> *[T]here is nothing better for people than to be happy and to do good while they live. That each of them may eat and drink, and find satisfaction in all their toil— this is the gift of God.*
> —Eccles. 3:12–13 (NIV)

God defines happiness for us. But for many, the idea of happiness is applied by avoiding adversity and setbacks. Our culture, for example, sets out to achieve happiness by steering clear of anything that could ruin the progression of our quality of life. That is why my mom and dad parented the way they did. In their battle to prevent hardship, they raised me to succeed in life—not to fail—because failure might produce unhappiness. That is how my parents thought. If they could achieve success in every aspect of life, they knew that would make them happy. In theory, their happiness would enable them to raise happy children. That would also bring my grandparents' joy. In that scenario, everyone ends up happy—Grandpa, Grandma, Mom, Dad, the kids, and the whole household. That's not a bad approach. I mean, who doesn't want a completely happy family? Who doesn't want to live without conflict and strife? Everybody wants a happy home with successful people thinking happy thoughts and doing happy things. But here's how that approach gets tricky. Grandma's and Grandpa's definitions of happiness and success differ from Mom's and Dad's definitions of happiness and success. Also, Mom's and Dad's ideas of happiness and success might not resemble my idea of happiness and success.

Different definitions of happiness within a family unit won't holistically align. That is a fact we all must face. Each family member ends up having to accept each other's definitions of happiness. This is probably where we get the phrase, "I'm happy if you're happy." My dad, for example, wanted me to either go to college after my senior year or join the military. If I was going to remain in his house, I *had* to have a job, essentially work and go to school. He thought that providing me with a place to live while I worked all day and studied all night would make me happy. But what actually would have made me happy was if he had just paid for my schooling and let me live at home for free. That way I wouldn't have to work. I could go to classes, study a little, relax, and play video games. Well, that was never going to happen, so I compromised. By joining the Marines, my dad would be happy with me that I was taking adult responsibility toward success. And I'd be happy not working at a minimum wage job while drowning in schoolwork.

If I'd been a Christian at that time, I wonder how different my decision might have been. If I had known God was the originator of happiness, would I have prayed about what to do? Where would God have guided me? I wasn't a believer yet, so I never thought to ask what God wanted. Looking back and knowing what I know now, I wish I would have consulted the Lord. I know he gave me the freedom to choose, but I still would have liked to know what he wanted. My choice wasn't an act of faith; it was simply the logical thing to do. I needed my parents' approval, and I had a baby on the way. Joining the Marines made sense. I needed to stand on my own two feet and try to be happy, but I also wanted to appease my parents. I didn't want them to resent me. If I had procrastinated, that might have sown discord between us. So I did what I thought was best for me *and* my parents, a compromise born out of passive aggression.

When husbands apply this idea of compromise to their marriage relationship, it translates to "happy wife, happy life." That's not necessarily a bad thought. Husbands should want to make their wives happy. But the meaning of that phrase is a cultural one. It is widely accepted by men who simply allow women to get their way so life can be easy. That seems logical. But let's go back to the Garden of Eden. Does "happy wife, happy life" resemble too much of what happened in the fall? Adam stood by the tree as Eve got her way. He watched her partake of what God prohibited. Instead of gently grabbing Eve's hand and lovingly turning her away from the tree, Adam chose the path of least resistance. Instead of gazing into her eyes and reminding her of the beautiful life they already had—even without the forbidden fruit—he chose not to step in. That would have been the perfect moment for Adam to be a hero. It was the perfect opportunity for him to stand against the schemes of Satan, clutch that snake by the neck, throw it on the ground, and smash its head with his foot. That is most certainly what God would have wanted.

Happiness in life is a byproduct of fully trusting in what God wants. Happiness in marriage is a byproduct of never "eating from the tree" that is off limits. God's idea of happiness is for every couple to be satisfied in his sovereignty, and to be fully captivated by his idea of life and love. It's obvious that Satan had a different agenda, and Adam and Eve ended up trading a king's paradise for the devil's playground. They chose dust-ridden thorns and thistles over green pastures and still waters. When they ate from the tree, the perfect form of human happiness was stripped from the world. From that day forward, human happiness was tainted throughout every generation. Complete joy now lacks its cornerstone, a void that only Jesus can fill.

In the case of Adam, "happy wife, happy life" brought him and his wife into a state of guilt and shame. In the case of Adam, when Eve got her way, it brought pain and suffering into their marriage. It resulted in a life that was no longer free from sin, a life now marked by sadness. This sad condition can only be remedied by the originator of happiness. It can only be cured by a plan of redemption that Jesus carried out to restore innocence and true joy. The cure was when Jesus was crucified on the cross. He gave up his own life to bring everlasting joy into the world. It's remarkable how the tragic death of an innocent man (Jesus) is the key to bringing unspeakable joy to so many. That should speak volumes to us about how God the Father deeply cares for his sons and daughters. God has gone to the greatest lengths to ensure the happiness of his children. Knowing this, we can conclude that God not only takes extreme measures to bring us happiness but also intends for us to remain in a state of happiness forever.

> [T]hose the LORD has rescued . . . will enter Zion with singing; everlasting joy will crown their heads. Gladness and joy will overtake them, and sorrow and sighing will flee away.
>
> —Isa. 35:10 (NIV)

Happiness Is a Priority to God

God's Word is where we get our definition and idea of happiness. So, to all husbands wanting to make their wives happy, do it! But do it considering the joy that God provides. And for every wife looking to keep her man happy, do it! But do it in a way that aligns with the promises of God's Word. God loves it when married men and women are genuinely happy together. Genuinely happy spouses make genuinely happy houses. Those happy houses are empowered to produce genuinely happy families. Those happy families contribute to the genuine happiness of churches, neighborhoods, schools, communities, and even entire cities. Genuine happiness spreads like wildfire, especially when it is achieved by the people of God. Everyone—whether they'll admit it or not—wants to be genuinely happy. But they'll need Christ to attain it.

In the same way that we extend God's peace and love, we extend the good news of the joy he provides.

> You make known to me the path of life; in your presence there is fullness of joy; at your right hand are pleasures forevermore.
>
> —Ps. 16:11

In the same way that we should share the gospel, we are to share and spread his joy to others.

> *I have told you these things so that my joy may be in*
> *you and your joy may be complete.*
> —John 15:11 (CSB)

When the joy of Jesus is in us, our joy can be made complete. When the happiness of God consumes us, our happiness can be made whole. The Bible says plenty about happiness being an important strength for your marriage. The first example we've touched on already is the story of Adam and Eve. Scripture reveals in the first two chapters of Genesis that God created a happy environment for life and love. God gladly gave Adam everything. He set him up for complete success. Adam had the most amazing food and an incredible lifestyle. He had the highest of leadership roles. Nothing on earth had dominion over him. God made Adam CEO on his first day at work, and the view from his workplace was pristine. It had a gorgeous river and phenomenal trees. With every spectacular sunrise and breathtaking sunset, the weather always had a perfect feel. The air's fragrance was that of the finest perfume. Abundant resources were available to Adam. He had the finest gold and the most precious stones. He also had the freedom to create a recreational palace. He had the best fishing spots and vast amounts of wood to build boats, piers, log cabins, and anything he wanted.

Then God gave him a stunning bride to share it all with. He brought him a beautiful woman to share his happiness with. He protected Adam from loneliness by giving him a better half to make him whole. For Adam's emotional health and sanity, God provided him with a companion of the opposite sex. In doing so, he protected him from things that were "not good" (Gen. 1:18) or not happy. Things were very good with the start of a loving relationship, a moment of romance, and—it's important to note—a heterosexual union. This was the perfect picture of the beginning of human happiness, a husband and a wife sharing life—the only union capable of continuing the human race for generations to come.

The natural relationship between man and woman (male and female) was designed to further define true human happiness. It is the catalyst by which life was able to continue from the first couple to the first child to the first family. When Christians decide to become spouses, they participate in the life-giving joy that is representative of Jesus faithfully holding fast to his church. When the saints make a lifelong commitment to marital unity, a beautifully joined happiness takes place that reflects the oneness of the Body of Christ. This beautifully joined happiness is to be kept sacred. It is to be protected with the law of God, which is holiness, and the law of Christ, which is love.

I like to think that's why God put certain statutes in place for married couples. For Adam and Eve, it was this:

> And the LORD God commanded the man, saying, "You may surely eat of every tree of the garden, but of the tree of the knowledge of good and evil you shall not eat, for in the day that you eat of it you shall surely die."
>
> —Gen. 2:16–17

This is God's first piece of perfect guidance and all-knowing wisdom. It qualifies as Adam's first premarital counseling session because God instructs him on how to keep his future wife safe and out of harm's way. By making him aware of the potential danger to society, Adam is given everything he needs to preserve his life and the life of his bride. Within this statute, God introduces two key elements to happiness: faithfulness and trust. Any unfaithful act or betrayal of trust would surely ruin Adam and Eve's happiness. As we know, that's exactly what happened. The moment they broke their allegiance to God, all hell broke loose. The instant they joined the devil's schemes, they were filled with pain and regret. That pain and regret would alter the course of their lives *and* their marriage forever. There was no longer perfect peace, and things were no longer "very good." Their happy environment was disrupted entirely.

We must understand that before Adam and Eve's disobedience, married life was a perfectly joyous experience. But their fully charged partnership was drained by the mother of all mistakes. Their perfect happiness was diminished by humiliation when Adam was passive and Eve was unable to resist temptation. Both of their hearts broke, and their minds suffered when they missed the mark. This produced frightful emotions like insecurity and dismal confusion. Eve's doubt and Adam's blame gave birth to the existence of marital stress and disorder.

The fall of humankind leaves us with a plethora of takeaways. One of them is if you want to be happy, be faithful to God and always trust him. Another one is this: If you want a happy marriage, be faithful to your spouse and build lifelong trust between the two of you. In the Bible, we find how important this is to God. Here's another example from an Old Testament verse you don't hear very often:

> When a man is newly married, he shall not go out with the army or be liable for any other public duty. He shall be free at home for one year to be happy with his wife whom he has taken.
>
> —Deut. 24:5

I know what you're thinking, probably the same thing I thought when I read that verse. Who can afford to take a 12-month staycation? I'm not sure my wife could put up with me for even 12 *days* in a row, let alone 12 *months* (just kidding). When Brittany and I look at this verse, we think about the many benefits of getting away together throughout the year. Every month we commit to sharing moments without distraction. It does wonders for our marriage. Time alone together reminds us that our careers will never be as important to us as we are to each other. It reminds us that our biggest investment is our lives together. Time away as a couple strengthens our desire to be united. It confirms that our highest priority (besides God) and greatest gift (besides Jesus) are each other. For me as a minister, it attests to the fact that my ministry starts with her. She comes before any disciple or mentee, and she is more important than any fellow leader or pastor.

This verse also says that at the start of your marriage, you should work together toward a strong foundation. When a man is newly married, he should zero in on his commitment to his wife, and vice versa. There should be a healthy focus on making sure your relationship with your spouse is solid. Happiness helps husbands and wives build a strong foundation, so it makes sense for them to have opportunities to be free at home as often as possible. It is wise to devote time and energy to your spouse without working too many long hours or taking excessive business trips, for example. Developing a pattern of pouring into each other preliminarily aligns with God's original plan for a happy, peaceful marriage.

But just because you start off spending all your free time together doesn't necessarily mean it will be peachy. There's nothing magical about being intentional for exactly one year. It's not like you put your time in and then, abracadabra, your marriage is perfect. However, 12 months is plenty of time for spouses to build foundational love that lasts. It's also ample enough time to experience conflict. When you and your spouse are living under the same roof, inevitably there will be friction. You will encounter bumps in the road. While on the same path, it's important to know how to navigate through the not-so-smooth terrain.

During my first year of marriage to Brittany, I didn't know exactly how to reconcile our differences. We went through some strife and hit a few potholes. But she loved me to death and knew God had a plan for us to stay on course. She helped us stay in motion as no other woman could. Witnessing firsthand my flaws made her more aware of the sins I was battling. It also provided her with the opportunity to relate to my struggle, to be strong when I was weak. And Brittany knew she had weaknesses too. She knew she had some soul-searching to do during that rough patch. Through prayer and confession, God helped us end our disputes. We both owned up to our stuff and admitted our faults to each other. That produced forgiveness and humility in our marriage.

Forgiveness and humility are two awesome characteristics of God. Forgiveness is a great contributor to a loving home and a peaceful atmosphere. Humility enables love to cover a multitude of sins, which creates a culture of grace—a culture that Jesus sacrificed himself for. Think about that the next time you're about to explode on your spouse. Think about it next time the conversation gets heated and verbal shots are fired. Husbands, when you get fed up with her, remember that Jesus sacrificed himself for your wife. Remember what you are called to do.

> *Husbands, love your wives, as Christ loved the church and gave himself up for her.*
> —Eph. 5:25

Wives, when he's acting like a complete jerk, remember that Jesus sacrificed himself for your husband. Remember that you are a follower of Christ.

> *Likewise, wives, be subject to your own husbands, so that even if some do not obey the word, they may be won without a word by the conduct of their wives, when they see your respectful and pure conduct.*
>
> —1 Pet. 3:1–2

This idea of cultivating grace between you and your spouse has the power to protect your marriage from tremendous fallout. Grace, when applied biblically, is highly contagious. It is essential for you and your spouse. Like genuine happiness, grace has the potential to spread like wildfire. It is necessary for unity within your home, your neighborhood, your church, and your city. Grace affects other couples in your area. It influences other marriages close by and transforms families. Grace is so vital that we'll spend the entire next chapter discussing what it is, where it comes from, and how to apply it. Keep yourselves in the joy of your Deliverer, and know this:

> *Happy are the people whose God is the LORD!*
>
> —Ps. 144:15 (NKJV)

Chapter 7

A Culture of Grace

What do you think of when you hear the word *grace*? If you're from the South, grace is prayer time before supper. We bless the meal by "saying grace." For the visual artist, grace is used to describe tones and contours that are pleasing to the eye. In professional dancing, grace is an emotion that is felt and expressed. A ballerina with grace in her body can elegantly stand on the tips of her toes. To some, grace is just a name—Grace Jones, Grace Kelly, Nancy Grace, Topher Grace, Will and Grace. To others, it doesn't mean anything.

There was a time when grace didn't mean a whole lot to me. It was just a name. My stepdaughter's middle name is Grace. When she's in trouble, my wife will say, "Dakota Grace!" Sometimes when we're being silly, we'll call her Gracie Lou after Sandra Bullock's character in *Miss Congeniality*. The first person I met with the name Grace was an aunt on my mother's side. We call her Aunt Gracie. And since I'm a sports fan, I grew up watching

Mark Grace, a Major League athlete. He played first base for the Chicago Cubs back in the late '80s and early '90s. As a movie buff, I once came across a film called *Amazing Grace and Chuck*. It's a story about a nuclear weapons protest, and it's also from the late '80s. That was the first time I heard the phrase *amazing grace*. But it wasn't until years later that I heard the famous song. You know the one. It starts like this:

> Amazing grace
> How sweet the sound
> That saved a wretch like me
> I once was lost
> But now I'm found
> Was blind, but now I see.

Today, there are few songs more beautiful than "Amazing Grace." For me, few songs are more meaningful. But that wasn't always so. I remember hearing "Amazing Grace" decades ago and initially thinking how powerful it was. It sounded like an old hymn from a past generation. It resembled a choir song, one you'd hear during a traditional Presbyterian service or after a Baptist Sunday sermon. I didn't quite get the lyrics. I didn't know why amazing grace sounded so sweet. I never knew what a wretch was, and at the time, I had no concept of being spiritually lost—only physically lost. I also didn't know what it meant to be spiritually blind—only physically blind. The second verse wasn't much easier to comprehend.

> 'Twas grace that taught my heart to fear
> And grace my fears relieved
> How precious did that grace appear
> The hour I first believed.

It wasn't until I became a Christian that I learned about grace and understood why it is so amazing.

What Is Grace?

When defining what grace is, it's important to know what grace isn't. Grace is not accidental; it is always intentional. Grace comes with love. It comes with truth. Grace is not earned, it is given, and it is given freely. Grace is a gift that keeps on giving. When God gives us grace, he reveals his compassion for us. Grace brings peace *with* God and reconciliation *to* God. Grace is divine intervention that works in us. It is not passive. It is very much active. Grace is a catalyst for transformation.

Grace is how the life of a former slave trader named John Newton was transformed. Newton, a renowned evangelist and clergyman, beloved husband, and father, wrote the song "Amazing Grace" in the late 1700s. But before he penned one of the greatest hymns ever written, Newton was a shockingly immoral man. He made a mockery of God through his former lifestyle and seemed the type of person farthest from being born again. But as the song says, it was *grace* that taught his heart to fear, and *grace* his fears relieved. That's such a beautiful verse. What an appropriate truth to sing to God because without grace, our hearts can't be taught to fear God. Scripture speaks about how fundamental it is to live in awe of our Maker.

> *The fear of the LORD is the beginning of wisdom, and the knowledge of the Holy One is insight.*
> —Prov. 9:10

The fear spoken of in this proverb is not the common form of fear that burdens people with anxiety, doubt, and worry. No, it is a healthy fear. To fear God means to trust him and trust his plan for your life. When grace teaches your heart to fear, you learn how to get on your knees and pray to God; you learn how to acknowledge him as Creator and revere him as King. As you meet with God in this way, you commune with him. And as you commune with him, he graciously gives you *wisdom* and *insight*. Wisdom enables you to see grace for what it is: undeserved favor.

That's what John Newton had in mind when he wrote "Amazing Grace." It was *wisdom* that showed him what a wretch he was and *insight* that informed him of his need to be saved. Newton was lost, and God found him. He was blind, and God made him see. Once Newton's eyes were opened, grace turned him from a life of blasphemy to a life of ministry. God poured out amazing grace on a rebellious slave ship captain and turned him into a prominent pastor. John Newton got to spend his latter days living for the gospel. His life became devoted to the message of God's kindness, a kindness he knew he did not deserve. Grace taught him to marvel at God's ability to apprehend his heart and captivate his soul. It also taught him gratitude, an attribute he expressed in the third verse of his song.

> Through many dangers, toils, and snares
> I have already come
> 'Tis grace hath brought me safe thus far
> And grace will lead me home.

John Newton was grateful to God for many things. One example was how God kept him safe. Newton once had a near-death experience in the middle of the ocean. During a frightful storm that was sure to seal his fate, God spared his life. Instead of letting him die on a sinking boat, God rescued him and transformed him into a vessel of mercy. "Amazing Grace" is a song of remembrance and testimony, a reflection of the unmerited favor that all Christians receive.

> The Lord has promised good to me
> His Word my hope secures
> He will my Shield and Portion be
> As long as life endures.

Grace is God's active love made available for those who don't deserve it. Grace is God moving mountains and tearing down walls to rescue sinners who would never be able to rescue themselves. Grace is freedom for the guilty ones at the ultimate sacrifice of the Innocent One, Jesus. John Newton was aware of that, and he never forgot it. He became an ambassador for Christ, a herald for the cross. He became a messenger for the man—Jesus—who takes away the sins of the world, the author and perfecter of our faith. John Newton was a servant. He was a follower of the way, the truth, and the life. Grace was evident in his marriage through his love for his wife. It was manifest in his parenting through his affection for his kids. And it was obvious in his preaching through endless devotion to his church.

We Need Grace

If you and your spouse are avid churchgoers, you've heard your fair share of sermons on grace. Preachers today regularly encourage husbands and wives to have grace for other people and to give grace as well. This idea comes from the Bible. Grace is a constant theme throughout the Old and New Testaments. In every book of the Bible, literally from Genesis to Revelation, we are shown that God is a giver of grace. God has tremendous grace for his people. Grace was given to Adam and Eve. It was given to Noah and his wife. Abraham and Sarah received grace from God, and so did

Moses and Zipporah, Boaz and Ruth, David and Bathsheba, and so on. God's grace has consistently been made available to couples. In generations past, it has helped countless husbands and wives, including Joseph and Mary, Jesus's parents.

Grace was given to Manoah and his once-barren wife, the mother of Samson. Grace was given to the prophet Hosea and his wife of whoredom, Gomer. Through all these Bible stories, God extended grace to the people who followed him, but he also made grace available to the husbands and wives who turned their backs on him. Some of them made huge mistakes. God was gracious to those who were faithful and gracious to those who were poor decision-makers. In all instances, God allowed them to come as they were but loved them enough to not let them remain as they were. When you surrender your life to Jesus, God's grace allows you to come as you are, but it never lets you remain as you are. Grace is the ultimate game-changer.

> *For by grace you have been saved through faith. And this is not your own doing; it is the gift of God, not a result of works, so that no one may boast.*
>
> —Eph. 2:8–9

Grace removes the argument that we can take any credit for getting right with God. Grace says we are entitled to nothing good, yet God gives us everything good. It tells us we deserve nothing the Lord provides, yet he still provides it. All we deserve is punishment for our sins. But God gives us the exact opposite— salvation, redemption, mercy, and forgiveness. That is why it is called the gift of God. That is why we call it amazing grace.

If you and your spouse are believers, that means you are the recipients of the gift of God. You and your spouse have received amazing grace, and now you are stewards of grace. That means you receive grace, you give grace, and you extend grace upon grace to others, especially your spouse. It's important to remember that all couples need grace. Every marriage and every spouse needs grace. But "having grace" is not merely accepting your spouse for who they are and "giving grace" is not simply accepting your spouse for *how* they are. It involves partnering to work through each other's "stuff"—things like mood swings, short fuses, pet peeves, and pushed buttons. Husbands and wives should be prepared for their ideologies to clash and for their differences to make waves. Along with that is the possibility of being a couple with unpaired levels of spiritual maturity. When a man and woman are joined together, the odds are that one spouse's faith is stronger than the others. Or perhaps one spouse's relationship with God is healthier than the others. No one's marriage is going to be a perfect expedition. But every couple who allows God's grace to guide them will gain marital excellence along the way.

We are all dependent on God's grace, and that's a good thing because marriage can get messy. Dealing with a messy marriage is often overwhelming. When you're not able to get on the same page with your spouse for whatever reason, that can produce unwanted stress. When my marriage got messy, I noticed that the stress crept into other areas of my life. For example, when my wife and I fought, it distracted me from my faith. I couldn't have a morning quiet time when I was angry at my wife. My attitude was such that I didn't want to do anything spiritual. Bible study became next to impossible because I couldn't concentrate.

Work was also an area that was affected. When I went to work after arguing with my wife, I was completely distracted by it. I couldn't be the normal warm and friendly businessman my clients knew. It was hard to be kind to coworkers as well. I ended up faking my way through the day. Then when I got home, the stress was waiting for me on my doorstep. As soon as I walked inside, my kids became targets for airing out my frustrations. I scolded the older ones for not keeping their rooms clean and yelled at the toddler for leaving his toys everywhere. There was even a time when my youngest, Baby Jack, fell under the wrath of my frustration.

One evening, I had just changed Jack's diaper, and not even a few minutes later he pooped all over himself again. It was really stinking up the house. Brittany was busy doing something else, so I picked him up and stomped off to the changing table. Right when I laid him down, he started wiggling, trying to roll over on his stomach. "Be still!" I yelled, trying to remove his diaper. This was a nasty one. It was leaking soupy poop out the sides. Jack kept wanting to roll over. "No, Jack!" I yelled again to get him to cooperate. I tried to restrain him with my free hand, but he didn't like that one bit. He got fussy and started to whine. I finally got his diaper open. The smell intensified so much that I couldn't decide if I should hold my breath or breathe through my mouth. Just then, Jack grabbed the poop diaper and flung it out from underneath him. You can guess which expletive I yelled next. It was so loud that it scared Jack and made him cry. My step kids came running down the hall. "What happened?" they asked. "Nothing! Go to your room!" I said. I was so angry that I didn't even let them help with the awful mess.

Just when I thought this crappy situation couldn't get any worse, I saw that the wipes and fresh diapers were totally out of my reach. By that time, the nasty, stinky, soupy poop diaper was all over the carpet. Jack continued to cry. He had poop all over his butt, his leg, and his hand. I just stood there defeated. That's when conviction hit me. I felt ashamed at that moment—ashamed that I was blaming my wife for not being available to do this, ashamed that I had taken it out on my step kids and mistreated Jack for something he had no control over.

By the grace of God, I was able to take a deep breath and regain my composure. I carefully got Jack in the bathtub and rinsed him off. I grabbed some toys near the bathroom and kept the water running. Jack knew where this was headed, so he calmed down a bit. He started clapping his hands as I filled the tub with soap bubbles. The smile on his face as he splashed around helped me realize what a jerk I'd been. Conviction hit me again because nothing I was doing about the stress of my marriage or the complications of home life was helping build a culture of grace. I was actually ripping it down. When that hit, I knew the Holy Spirit was speaking to me. I knew grace upon grace was being poured out because it's not natural for me to think that way. I needed divine help, and the Word of God was there to set me free from my sinful tendencies.

> *[W]alk in a manner worthy of the calling to which you have been called, with all humility and gentleness, with patience, bearing with one another in love, eager to maintain the unity of the Spirit in the bond of peace.*
>
> —Eph. 4:1–3

I was called to be a humble man, a gentle husband, and a patient father. At that moment, I wasn't being any of those. I wasn't bearing with my wife in love or eager to maintain the unity of the Spirit in the bond of peace. All I cared about was convenience and control. I lied to myself about not deserving this type of predicament. I thought I was entitled to a life of ease—a fool's mistake at best. God's grace helped me see that instead of cleaning up the mess, I had been contributing to it. Instead of putting out the fire, I was fueling it. I wasn't remedying anything. I'd forgotten that the first step in providing a solution is knowing

I am part of the problem. In dealing with Jack and his soupy poop diaper, I saw how unreasonable I was with him. After all, he was just a baby and babies pee and poop all over themselves. As his father, it's my responsibility to approach that situation with reason and preparedness. That means I make sure I have an ample supply of wipes, diapers, rash cream, and everything I'll need to keep him clean. As he grows and develops, he'll learn to use the potty and keep himself clean. But I need to be there every step of the way to walk him through it.

Sometimes we can be unreasonable with our spouses. They're not perfect, and we shouldn't expect them to be because that's unreasonable. Our spouses are going to sin against us, and we're going to sin against them. There will be times of letdown and disappointment on both sides. We must never forget that we are all saved by amazing grace. It is our responsibility to approach our messy marriages with reason and preparedness. That means we make sure we have an ample supply of love and forgiveness, mercy and grace, patience and understanding. God provides everything we need to keep our marriage clean. And he will be there every step of the way to help husbands and wives walk through the mess together.

Marital Health Is Propelled by Grace

There's a passage of Scripture that came to mind as I was putting this chapter together. It's in Matthew 18, the section called the Parable of the Unforgiving Servant. There, Jesus says it's not only seven times that you forgive others but seventy times seven. In context, the parable is used by Jesus to further describe the full functionality of church discipline. He teaches us that because God has forgiven our sins, we are to never withhold forgiveness from those who seek it. We are to forgive debts the same way he forgave our debt. We are to show mercy to others in the same way he has shown mercy to us. Jesus drives the point home that Christians are to be the model of loving, forgiving, and merciful people. And we are to do that over and over again.

As I read that passage, I found myself thinking about my relationships, in particular, my relationship with my wife because sometimes I withhold forgiveness from her. Sometimes I'm not ready to be merciful because of how she "offended me." Sometimes, I'm not ready to make up out of fear that she might not "learn her lesson." When my mind goes there, it reveals that I've forgotten I've been forgiven of an enormous amount of sin. As a Christian husband, that sets a bad example for my wife. I ponder why Jesus tells us to forgive each other 490 times over. There's nothing magical about that number. Why would he say that? I believe Jesus knew that when we commit to acknowledging what we did wrong and seek to make it right, that creates a space for humility in our lives. Then when we forgive each other again and again (like he forgives us), it creates room for love to cover a massive number of shortcomings. When we can overlook minor offenses with respect again and again, that creates a culture of grace.

When we can pick our battles in step with the Spirit, we can be kind and gentle, patient and understanding. We can be gracious peacemakers. And by the time we've forgiven our spouse 490 times over, our marriage is that much stronger. How? Because grace is a catalyst for transformation. And as grace transforms our hearts, the outward demonstration of our faith begins to inspire other couples out there struggling. Grace gives those who are without hope reason to inquire of the light inside of us, shining brightly for them to see. God gives us grace because he cares for our marriages and the marriages around us. As we receive God's grace, we must anticipate sharing it with others. Christian husbands and wives show the world they care by laying down a foundation of mercifulness.

Grace might sound like a catalyst for a free ride, but it's not. It doesn't enable smooth sailing. It's not a means for couples to coast through life. Grace doesn't mean we don't confront our spouse. It doesn't mean we sweep our mess under the rug and ignore complications within our marriage. Going back to Matthew 18, that passage also has a section about dealing with sin. Jesus says the following:

> *If your brother sins against you, go and tell him his fault, between you and him alone. If he listens to you, you have gained your brother.*
>
> —Matt. 18:15

Remember, this portion of Scripture is about the directive and prescription for church discipline. However, if you live with the mindset that each Christian home functions like a mini church with the husband shepherding the flock, it's easy to apply this passage to your marriage. God uses our spouse to lovingly call us out on our sins. He enables each husband to see his wife's faults and vice versa. If I sin against my wife, I want her to come and tell me my fault, just the two of us alone. In doing so, she keeps me accountable and informs me of things that go right over my head. If I listen to her, she has gained me as a husband, a true confidant, and a lifelong companion. Couples should be equipped to plant seeds in each other's hearts so God can water them for growth and gain. That gain is essential in the cultivation of grace culture. The intent of that gain is love, unity, and peace. It's not so husbands can "keep their wives in check," and it's not so wives can "steamroll their husbands." It's so every married man and woman can continue together in harmony for the glory of God.

> *For we are his workmanship, created in Christ Jesus*
> *for good works, which God prepared beforehand, that*
> *we should walk in them.*
>
> —Eph. 2:10

Grace reminds us that we are his workmanship created for good works. Grace is not meant for spouses to permanently tolerate each other's old self but rather to further progress the new self. I thank God for that. If grace had been intended for my wife to tolerate my chauvinism, she'd be one oppressed woman. If grace was intended for her to put up with my addictions, she'd be one lonely partner. If grace was intended for her to overlook my mean-hearted ways, she'd be one miserable bride.

Grace Empowers Lifelong Marriage

For all husbands and wives who receive grace, God intends to make them more like Jesus. The Scriptures tell us this:

> *[P]ut off your old self, which belongs to your former*
> *manner of life and is corrupt through deceitful desires*
> *. . . and . . . be renewed in the spirit of your minds . . .*
> *and . . . put on the new self, created after the likeness*
> *of God in true righteousness and holiness.*
>
> —Eph. 4:22–24

When we become Christians, there is a former manner of life that we let go of and a new way of life that we embrace. When Christians get married, that new way of life continues. But being married doesn't necessarily make that pursuit easier. It can actually make it a lot tougher. Sharing your life with someone else is hard work. Here's another way to say that: working together to become more like Jesus in true righteousness and holiness is a difficult responsibility. But it's not the grace of God that makes it tough. It is our lack of understanding of what God's grace is that causes us trouble. If you want your marriage to work, you must understand how the grace of God works.

During the first year of my marriage to Brittany, it was obvious I had lost sight of a lot of things. One of those things was the doctrine of grace. For a while, I think I had a blurred understanding and a vague remembrance of how I came to know Christ. By default, I forgot how to have grace for others and how to give grace to others, especially my wife. Grace had become a loose term that was easy to sing about in church but so easy to take for granted the rest of the time. That was dangerous for me because when I lost sight of grace, I lost sight of what I had been saved from. And when the severity of what I had been saved from escaped me, the enemy saw an opportunity to attack my marriage. I was enticed to push the envelope with the freedom of marital intimacy. I had a selfish craving to "enhance" our sex life. I thought if Brittany would allow certain things, it might heighten our marital experience and bring us closer together intimately. I'm so glad she refused all of it because where does a dark desire like that end once you go down that road? The answer is that it never ends. The next thing you know, you start convincing yourself that whatever "enhancements" you're making are not enough. You'll want more; you'll need more. By then you've opened yourself up to more possibilities, and the enemy floods your mind with endless options. Eventually, you might end up with multiple partners in your sex life, for example.

Grace never involves extramarital relations. Some spouses get tempted to ease the difficulty of staying together by letting mistresses and lovers into their bedrooms. But grace does not permit things like open marriage or a "hall pass," for example. Anyone who might not know what a hall pass is, it is a week off from marriage to do whatever you want without consequences. Yes. I know it's hard to believe, but such a thing exists. Some spouses actually make temporary agreements to relax monogamy to relieve stress and restlessness within marriage. I'm not one to judge and I've done far worse in previous relationships, but hall passes are disgusting, and in my opinion, they defeat the purpose of being married and attack the work of God in relationships.

Why am I telling you this? Because God's grace is a shield against such temptation and distorted thinking. God's grace has the power to keep sexual sin from ever entering your marriage. If you're already struggling, it has the power to restore the marital union. It can keep separation from arising and divorce off the table. Grace can also prevent the flame of marital love between a husband and a wife from burning out, and here's why. It's because it doesn't permit either spouse to ignore their partner's setbacks— things like backsliding and spiritual regression. When a culture of grace is built between two spouses, it does not allow for a husband or a wife to remain in their pit. Grace doesn't leave you stagnant in your faith. As grace is extended from one spouse to another, it serves as empowerment for positive change, just as in the case of your salvation.

> God, who is rich in mercy, because of his great love that he had for us, made us alive with Christ even though we were dead in our trespasses. You are saved by grace!
>
> —Eph. 2:4–5 (CSB)

In the same way God's grace saves sinners, God's grace saves spouses from tearing themselves apart. In the same way God's grace delivers us from the domain of darkness, God's grace rescues husbands and wives from "living hell" at home. Just as God gives grace to make us alive, spouses can give grace to breathe life into their marriages. What does that mean? Well, it means a lot of things. But primarily it means humbling yourself. It means saying you're sorry even when it's not your fault or saying you were wrong when you might have been right. It means asking for forgiveness first or offering forgiveness without being asked. It means going on a date night instead of going into the doghouse. It means using love language instead foul language. It means giving warm affection instead of a cold shoulder and holding hands instead of throwing the middle finger. Marriage doesn't thrive on who's right or wrong. It thrives on forgiveness. Marriage thrives on an overflow of amazing grace. No groom ever held onto his bride with his arrogance, and no wife makes a husband happy with her pride.

Humility is a pivotal building block for creating a culture of grace in marriage. We'll talk more about that in the next chapter.

Chapter 8

Humility Is Key

Warning! This might sound weird to you, but I love my wife's feet. I love her toes and her heels. I love caressing her feet, massaging them, and even kissing them. Her feet are soft and beautiful. She doesn't have much of an arch. In fact, her feet are flat. But she loves when I touch them and squeeze them. What's funny, though, is that she won't go anywhere near my feet. Feet gross her out. They make her gag, so she'll never understand my obsession. I don't blame her; my feet can get stinky. Throughout the workday, I spend a lot of time on my feet. My heels are crusty most of the time, so I get why she never rubs them. There's nothing sexy or appealing about my feet. I've never had a pedicure, but I do try to keep my toenails trimmed. One reason is that I like to wear flip-flops. Especially in the summer, you'll likely catch me in some type of open-toed shoes.

I believe in taking care of my feet and practicing good foot hygiene. No one should have to struggle with being grossed out by funky toes or unflattering toenails. That's just my opinion. I realize that foot hygiene can be a challenge for some people, but not for my wife. Her feet are gorgeous. They were one of the many physical features that drew me to her when we first started dating. Secretly, I couldn't wait to get my hands on them. That sounds like something a guy with a foot fetish would say. Okay, maybe. But at the time, Brittany was a single mom, one of the hardest jobs on the planet. She was co-parenting two kids and working a full-time gig. The last thing she needed was to have her feet neglected. Today, Brittany works 40-plus hours a week, and we now have more kids to chase around and clean up after. Most nights she ends up on the sofa, lying down with her legs on my lap while I rub her feet until my hands hurt. I love it. It's one of the many cherishable endings to my day. It reminds me of my devotion to her from her head to her toes.

The Lord's Feet

You're probably wondering where I'm going with all this foot talk. Just bear with me and keep reading. It'll all make sense, and everything will connect to marriage, I promise. We just need to dive into a little Bible study before we arrive at the point. There are a few memorable stories in the life of Jesus regarding touching feet. We all know the famous foot-washing story where Jesus cleans his disciples' feet the night before he's crucified. We'll have a chance to discuss that later in this chapter. For now, I'd like to draw your attention to a couple of other foot-washing stories involving women. The first is found in Luke's gospel. It's about an unnamed female who ends up at a social function where Jesus is.

When one of the Pharisees invited Jesus to have dinner with him, he went to the Pharisee's house and reclined at the table. A woman in that town who lived a sinful life learned that Jesus was eating at the Pharisee's house, so she came there with an alabaster jar of perfume. As she stood behind him at his feet weeping, she began to wet his feet with her tears. Then she wiped them with her hair, kissed them and poured perfume on them.

—Luke 7:36–38 (NIV)

I must admit that even for me (the guy who loves touching his wife's feet), this story seems strange. I can imagine being in the same room thinking, *Well, this is awkward, some random woman weeping all over Jesus's feet.* This isn't something you see every day. It must have been confusing to the onlookers. I've had some deep cries in my lifetime, some bad enough to shed a bowlful of teardrops. I could see how a weeping woman would be able to rinse her feet with her tears. But still, she'd have to be pretty darn close to Jesus for longer than a few minutes to wipe each foot with her hair. That would have surely drawn the attention of other guests and made a scene. In fact, it says in this passage that the Pharisee who was hosting thought it was highly inappropriate for Jesus to allow her to touch him. Jesus brought some clarity and informed everyone of what was really going on.

"Do you see this woman? I entered your house; you gave me no water for my feet, but she has wet my feet with her tears and wiped them with her hair. You gave me no kiss, but from the time I came in she has not ceased to kiss my feet. You did not anoint my head with oil,

but she has anointed my feet with ointment. Therefore I
tell you, her sins, which are many, are forgiven—for she
loved much." And he said to her, "Your sins are forgiven
. . . Your faith has saved you; go in peace."

—Luke 7:44–48, 50

Clearly, making a scene didn't matter to the woman. What mattered to her was getting her life right with the Lord and declaring her devotion to him. She walked in with clean hands and brushed hair, all done up and well put together. But she didn't leave that way. She left with redness in her eyes, icky hands, and frizzled dirty hair—a small price to pay to hear the words "your sins are forgiven." Wouldn't you agree? This woman was obviously without hope before she met Jesus. She knew she was a sinner, and she'd come to realize the depth of her wrongdoing. Her lifestyle was depressing to her. There was a void in her heart, and no matter what she did, it couldn't be filled. She was all alone and self-isolated until she found Jesus.

She knew religion couldn't save her. That's why she didn't wash the Pharisee's feet. She knew money wouldn't right her wrongs. That's why she didn't search for a rich guy to kiss. She didn't anoint a high-ranking politician in hopes of moving up in society; she knew that was a pipe dream. Instead, she sought a lowly teacher with dirty, smelly feet. And when she found him, the heavy burden of carrying all her sins, which were many, was lifted off her shoulders. Her "backpack full of bricks" was pulverized by Jesus, and the guilt in her heart was removed as far as the east is from the west. She arrived with shame, but because of Jesus, she carried on with confidence. She showed up in pain, but because of the Savior, she persevered in peace.

But what drew her to Jesus in the first place? It wasn't fancy clothes or a luxurious lifestyle. It wasn't a mansion or a grand estate. Jesus had none of that stuff. He didn't have a prestigious career or a hefty retirement plan. He didn't come from money. So what drew her to him? It wasn't his Middle Eastern good looks. No, it was the fact that he was a friend of sinners. Jesus stood out from all the other "religious" men of his day. He was preaching good news to poor people in a society where the impoverished were overlooked and neglected. He was teaching things like this:

> *Blessed are you who are poor, for yours is the kingdom of God. Blessed are you who are hungry, for you shall be satisfied. Blessed are you who weep now, for you shall laugh. Blessed are you when people hate you and when they exclude you. . . . Rejoice in that day, and leap for joy, for behold your reward is great in heaven.*
>
> —Luke 6:20–23

Jesus was both a man *of* the people and a man *for* the people. He had compassion on those in need, a compassion most sinners were told was unavailable to them. Most sinners thought they were stuck in a rut without any spiritual privileges. The sinful woman in this story categorized herself as unworthy of redemption. But then she heard of a great prophet who roamed the streets healing the blind, raising children from the dead, curing diseases, and cleansing lepers. She experienced the presence of God through the wondrous works of Jesus. She began to hope; she began to believe. She saw firsthand that Jesus was her answer. Then Jesus overcame her many sins with forgiveness. He overcame her wrongdoings with grace upon grace. This woman who lived a sinful life was drawn to Jesus's great humility, a key component of the gospel. With humility, Jesus captivates people's hearts and draws them in using incredible kindness and remarkable gentleness.

Here is my point in telling you this story. Fellas, if you want to draw your woman near to you, strive hard to be incredibly kind. If you want to bring your wife closer to you and keep her by your side, make an effort to be remarkably gentle. Don't try to fix your marriage with flowers and chocolates. The best tools for working on your relationship with your spouse are incredible kindness and remarkable gentleness. They reflect great humility. And since pride is your biggest enemy, humility must be your strongest ally. A proud man who humbles himself with the kindness of Jesus will demonstrate great love to his wife. Fill your marriage with the compassion of Jesus. Make time for meaningful conversations, date nights, romantic walks, and evenings by the fire. Bless your wife by being there for her. The woman in this story didn't want diamonds, lingerie, or sex. All she wanted was quality time with Jesus. She wanted to love much because of the man who loved her much.

Ladies, your husband is ongoingly responsible for drawing you to himself. As often as he can, he should be wooing you with humility. But when he can't or won't, remember that "your reward is great in heaven." That's where your hope is, not in your husband. Your hope isn't in your husband's ability but in the ability of your Lord and Savior. If your husband struggles to lead or lead well, that can put uncomfortable stress on your marriage. I know because Brittany struggled in the past due to my lack of leadership. Early in our marriage, I got busy and distracted. I got irresponsible, and as a result, my wife got overburdened with responsibility. I rarely helped out around the house or with the kids. I wasn't making time for Brittany, and that hurt our marriage.

If that happens to you, lovingly call your husband out. There's nothing wrong with humbly communicating your feelings. Just remember to do it with incredible kindness and remarkable gentleness. Like the woman in the story, fix your eyes upward on the prize found in Jesus. Forget what lies behind, and strain forward to what lies ahead (Phil. 3:13–14). Showing steadfast affection to your husband despite his past mistakes will reflect great humility. When a wife faithfully submits to the man she said "I do" to, it reveals that she has set her mind on things above where Jesus is (Col. 3:2).

Be Devoted to Each Other

I know that *submission* isn't a popular word these days. I know it doesn't sit well with our American culture. When we think of submission, we think of weakness. We associate the term *submission* with things that demean and belittle. Some people even think that the act of submission only applies to women, as if women are inferior to men. That is simply not true. We established in Chapter 3 of this book that the roles of men and women are complementary. Side by side, they are one in purpose—equal but different. Both sexes reflect God's image equally in their own unique way. But in marital union, husbands and wives reflect special truths about Jesus that they would not be able to on their own. One example is their oneness. Jesus mentioned this during his ministry.

> *For this reason a man will leave his mother and father and be united to his wife, and the two will become one flesh. So they are no longer two but one flesh. Therefore what God has joined together, let no one separate.*
>
> —Mark 10:7–9 (NIV)

In marriage, a man and a woman are joined together by God. This joining is so sacred that it should never be undone. God takes two equal but different parts that are whole and joins them to become one united whole in him. That oneness is representative of the oneness Jesus has with God. Jesus's oneness with God is inseparable. This oneness is what gave

Jesus the power to save us and make us one with him. And Jesus saved us knowing he would be crucified and put to death. He was that committed and submitted. Before going to the cross, Jesus humbly prayed this:

> *Father, if you are willing, take this cup [of death] from me; yet not my will, but yours be done.*
> —Luke 22:42 (NIV)

Every time we submit, we can be reminded of Jesus's submission. Think of it this way: Where would we be if Jesus hadn't lived a submissive life, submitting himself to God's will? What if he had rebelled as a child, dishonored his parents, and disrespected their authority over him? What if Jesus hadn't submitted to the officers who arrested him or the government that crucified him? At any point that Jesus was in trouble, he could have asked God to send an army of angels to protect him from injustice. Jesus had the divine power to fend off any man who tried to harm him. He had the power to bypass the soldiers who tortured him and crumble the empire that put him to death. Instead, he gave up his rights to carry out the plan of salvation for you and me. To submit means to express love and humility. It means to express devotion to something greater than yourself.

Husbands and wives need to know what it means to submit. Here is how the Bible defines submission in the context of marriage.

> *Wives submit to your husbands, as to the LORD, because the husband is the head of the wife as Christ is the head of the church. He is the Savior of the body. Now as the church submits to Christ, so also wives are to submit to their husbands in everything.*
> —Eph. 5:22–24 (CSB)

When the church submits to Jesus, it is a beautiful thing. In this context, what's being commanded is the pursuit of oneness through order and respect. To submit means the chance to participate in sacred unity. To submit means the opportunity to show the incredible kindness and remarkable gentleness of Jesus. Our submission renders God's glory and is a strong witness to nonbelievers. It shows everyone that God's Word is truth because it is the effect of genuine faith in Christ. It points to the teaching and example of Jesus. Here is what he said to his followers, both male and female, about how we are to submit.

> *You know that those who are regarded as rulers of the [people] lord it over them, and those in high positions act as tyrants over them. But it is not so among you. On the contrary, whoever wants to become great among you will be your servant, and whoever wants to be first among you will be a slave to all. For even the Son of Man did not come to be served, but to serve, and to give his life as a ransom for many.*
>
> —Mark 10:42–45 (CSB)

In a world full of people who crave control and long to be on top, Jesus says to lay all that down and be a servant. In a society where men are bossing women around and women are obsessing over girl power, Jesus says to be a slave to all. In relationships where love is a two-way street, Jesus says to sacrifice and serve. Instead of thinking of your marriage as give and take, God's Word says to think of it as give and give.

> *Be devoted to one another in love. Honor one another above yourselves.*
>
> —Rom. 12:10

*Do nothing out of selfish ambition or conceit, but
in humility consider others as more significant than
yourselves.*

—Phil. 2:3 (CSB)

When a wife submits to her husband, that is a beautiful
thing. There is love that is reflected and seen by all those in
her midst. When a husband counts his wife more significant
than himself and honors her above himself, that is a wonderful thing. It is evidence of God's grace in his life. It proves he
rejects secular ideology and accepts being transformed by the
Holy Spirit's renewing of his mind. Minds renewed with incredible kindness and remarkable gentleness, both male and
female, will take their marriage to places they never dreamed
possible. Couples who humble themselves together keep themselves together. Couples who keep themselves together with
humility position themselves for grace and set themselves up
to impact others.

The impact of other women is especially important to me
because it was their godly example that taught me kindness.
The impact of other men helped me understand that humility
is crucial for biblical manhood. The first time I got married, I
was 18 years old. Among the thousands of couples I've met over
the years, there are only a few who got hitched right out of high
school. Only a handful have been able to make their marriage last.
Those couples are special. It takes a lot of work to stay together
that long. It requires focus, maturity, and determination. Those
are all character traits I didn't possess at the age of 18. I knew
nothing about love—only lust. I had no concept of humility—
only pride. I never thought to serve my first wife; I just wanted
her to serve me. The only person I was devoted to was myself. I
wasn't giving my life to my first marriage or my first spouse. But

I sure did make her give everything in her life to me. It doesn't seem fair, does it? Our relationship was one-sided, and that's why she divorced me.

Be Devoted to Jesus

A woman is naturally born strong at heart. But when a man drains her of her strength, she's left with little energy to stick around. She can only put up with so much before she has to get out. That is one reason men must lead with humility. When Jesus was here on earth, he led with humility. Women's lives changed for the better because of him. Jesus energized women. He healed them and empowered them. He respected them and encouraged them. There were a significant number of women who gladly followed Jesus during his ministry. Many women believed in him and were devoted to him. One of those women was named Mary, Lazarus's sister. Lazarus was the guy Jesus brought back to life after he'd been deceased a few days. Mary was especially grateful for that miracle, and she showed it in her constant honoring of Jesus. Here's the story.

> *Six days before the Passover, Jesus came to Bethany, where Lazarus was, the one Jesus had raised from the dead. So they gave a dinner for him there; Martha was serving them, and Lazarus was one of those reclining at the table with him. Then Mary took a pound of perfume, pure and expensive nard, anointed Jesus's feet and wiped his feet with her hair. So the house was filled with the fragrance of the perfume.*
> —John 12:1–3 (CSB)

There was some controversy over whether or not Mary should have done this. Apparently, a few people thought the

expensive perfume could have been used for charitable purposes. They gave Mary a hard time for using it on Jesus's feet.
Here's how Jesus responded.

> *Why are you bothering this woman? She has done a*
> *beautiful thing for me. The poor you will always have*
> *with you, but you will not always have me. When she*
> *poured this perfume on my body, she did it to prepare*
> *me for burial. Truly I tell you, wherever this gospel is*
> *preached throughout the whole world, what she has*
> *done will also be told, in memory of her.*
>
> —Matt. 26:10–13 (NIV)

How marvelous! What I wouldn't give to hear Jesus say, "You
have done a beautiful thing for me." Mary knew who was in the
room—her Lord, her Messiah. She knew he was the Way, the
Truth, and the Life. In Mary's mind, anointing Jesus's feet with
thousands of dollars' worth of perfume was the least she could do
for her Savior. This was an act of pure worship, an unforgettable
picture of a devoted servant with her King. This was an act of pure
love, an awesome display of how God's precious daughters will
endear their Father in heaven forever.

Christian men and women should always be prepared to do
beautiful things for Jesus. My wife and I like helping the poor
and feeding the homeless. But we *love* doing it all in the name
of Jesus. Sometimes doing beautiful things are acts of kindness
such as helping the less fortunate. But sometimes doing beautiful
things might be sacrificing thousands of dollars for Jesus. For us
today, that might look like donating resources to the church or
funding a particular ministry devoted to God's work. The point is
that everything we do should be motivated by devotion to Jesus.
What we see in Mary's example is that devotion to Jesus reflects

great humility. As you devote yourself to Jesus, he guides you in making the best decisions. Allowing yourself to be led by him ensures the greatest amount of impact that your decision-making can produce. It brings positive change to people's lives, and it affects your own life.

All that applies directly to marriage. Devoting your life to Jesus develops a strong devotion in your heart toward your spouse. That is why the Scriptures say to love your spouse as Christ loves the church and gave himself up for her. Remember, we are the Bride of Christ. Jesus does wonderful things for his bride. He loves us so he made sacrifices for us. He cherishes us and nourishes our faith. He prays for us, and he stays with us. Let your marriage mirror the relationship that Jesus has with the Bride of Christ. Couples who cherish each other nourish each other's faith. Couples who pray together, stay together. Remembering all that Jesus has done for you catalyzes the spread of love in your marriage. The more time you spend at Jesus's feet, the more your love will impact your spouse. The more devoted you are to doing beautiful things for Jesus, the more your devotion will extend to your spouse.

Sometimes I get so caught up in my job and hobbies that I lose sight of doing beautiful things for Jesus. I misplace my devotion and forget that everything I do is supposed to flow from the gospel. Then, by default, I resort to going through the motions in all areas of life (my marriage, my church, and my parenting). I'm physically present but mentally absent. I'm there in the flesh but not all there in spirit. My mind transitions from being focused on heavenly things to obsessing about earthly things. When that happens, I tend to focus primarily on the here and now as it pertains to me.

I think that's how those guys who watched Mary anoint Jesus felt. At that moment, they cherished the pricy perfume instead of their Lord and Savior. It's revealed in their response.

When the disciples saw this, they were indignant.
"Why this waste?" they asked. "This perfume could
have been sold at a high price and the money given to
the poor."

—Matt. 26:8–9 (NIV)

During the busyness of life, sometimes we miss the obvious. It's in those moments that things go right over our heads, and it's the priority of earthly things that distract us. That's how I feel about the disciples in this story. They were too blind to see their Creator right in front of them. They were too proud to realize that nothing is ever wasted on Jesus, and they were too distracted to marvel at all the beautiful things he did for humanity. Had they not been caught up in their pride, they would have been first to kneel down and anoint Jesus's feet.

When the busyness of life happens to you, remember Mary's devotion. Let her testimony remind you of who you are and whose you are. Let it remind you that Mary's expensive perfume compares nothing to the great cost of what Jesus did for her. And let it be an ongoing reminder of what Jesus purchased for you at great cost—your name was written in the Book of Life, not in pencil but in permanent ink. It is confirmation of your permanent vacation to paradise. It's a dinner reservation to an endless feast at the Lord's table. With these truths, remind yourself that Jesus is worthy of all your prized possessions.

Even if you were to give Jesus everything you own—your house, your car, your finances—you would still be in debt to the immeasurable riches of his grace. But Jesus doesn't want your prized possessions. He doesn't want your stuff. He wants you to be devoted to God. He wants all husbands to be devoted to their marriage, even if their wives want out. He wants every wife to be devoted to her husband, even when she is mistreated or betrayed. Jesus wants all husbands and wives to love as he loves. And he wants you to love your spouse even when you aren't loved back. Do you agree? I hope so. There is a prime example in the Bible of what I'm talking about. And, yes, it has to do with feet.

> *The evening meal was in progress, and the devil had already prompted Judas, the son of Simon Iscariot, to betray Jesus. Jesus knew that the Father had put all things under his power and that he had come from God and was returning to God; so he got up from the meal, took off his outer clothing, and wrapped a towel around his waist. After that, he poured water into a basin and began to wash his disciples' feet, drying them with the towel that was wrapped around him.*
>
> —John 13:2–5 (NIV)

I love this. Jesus, the man of highest stature, elevated to the highest place and given the name above all names, performed a menial task reserved for low-ranking individuals. Jesus, the one by whom all things were created, used his all-powerful hands to wash dirty, stinky feet. The one in whom all the fullness of God was pleased to dwell stooped down to wipe filthy toes and clean dirty toenails. The King of kings and Lord of lords was also the Servant of servants. If that is not humility, then I don't know what is. If what he says next doesn't inspire us to be humble, then I don't know what will.

> *You call me Teacher and Lord—and you are speaking rightly, since that is what I am. So if I, your LORD and Teacher, have washed your feet, you also ought to wash one another's feet. For I have given you an*

example, that you also should do just as I have done for you. Truly I tell you, a servant is not greater than his master, and a messenger is not greater than the one who sent him. If you know these things, you are blessed if you do them.

—John 13:13–17 (CSB)

Did you catch that? If Jesus is your Lord and teacher, then the way he treats you is how you treat others. He has set the bar very high by going low. Keep in mind that this foot-washing ceremony was just hours before Judas would betray him. Jesus still treated Judas with respect by washing his feet clean. Jesus loved Judas until the end, and it was Judas who quit on their relationship. And every other disciple ran out on Jesus during his arrest—even Peter who denied Jesus three times. They left Jesus all alone; they abandoned him. But what waited for them on the other side of that betrayal was grace. What waited for Peter on the other side of mistreating Jesus was love. What waited for each disciple who ran out on Jesus was reconciliation. Sadly, Judas took his own life instead of reuniting with Jesus. The rest of the disciples, however, were forgiven because they humbled themselves.

Humility was essential for the people who followed Jesus, and it is essential for us. We're all sinners. There's no such thing as a sinner who doesn't sin. There are only sinners saved by perfect grace. None of us will have perfect marriages because there's no such thing as a perfect spouse. That means all imperfect spouses will get their feet dirty. And while Jesus is there to cleanse us, husbands and wives must also be there for each other's dirty feet. When marital conflict comes pounding on your door, let love and grace be waiting on the other side of it. When you and your spouse have a fight and someone is mistreated or disrespected, let grace be available for both parties to humble themselves and seek forgiveness.

When your marriage encounters a rough patch, let reconcilable love be available for each spouse to admit their mistake and apologize. Even if you need to get on your knees and "wash dirty feet," there is nothing beneath you when it comes to honoring your commitment to your spouse. Even when it's not your fault, you can take responsibility. If you need to say sorry first, so be it. Suffering for a little while to avoid pride—to avoid breaking someone's heart—is Christ-like. Jesus was crucified hand and foot for you to love your spouse and be devoted to them from head to toe. He says that couples who know these things are blessed if they do them.

Chapter 9

All In

During this life, agony and distress are constant among all people groups. The struggle of humanity is worldwide. Chaos is continual in most if not all countries. Global unity seems farther out of reach. Adversity is steadily on the horizon, and a great deal of tragedies strike each day. For some couples, there are more bad times than good. For some, the number of spouses being harmed in their communities is greater than the number of spouses being healed. The effect of this broken planet means being surrounded by an evil force that never sleeps. And in marriage, the influence of a fallen world lurks at our doorsteps. It sneaks into our homes, our living rooms, and our bedrooms. It takes its place at our kitchen tables. As a result, we experience conflict. Spouses collide with each other; tensions rise, and eventually, someone blows a gasket.

Not to minimize the reality of our broken planet or the brokenness that exists in us, but compared to heaven, we have reason to remain full of hope. For everything Jesus has done, we have enough reasons to remain full of joy. That is why it's good for husbands and wives to tell themselves God's truths. That is why I've spent the last eight chapters of this book reminding you of God's truths. Toward the end of the previous chapter, I mentioned that Jesus doesn't want your prized possessions. He doesn't want your stuff. It's true. Jesus wants your heart. To him, *you* are the prized possession. When you get saved, Jesus takes ownership of you in a way that is too beautiful to forget and too awesome to take for granted. Through the cross, he establishes a lifeline to your Deliverer. This lifeline makes way for a relationship with God in heaven, providing you with an inheritance that you bank on forever.

Hope for Your Future

Everyone in heaven will be well-off because God's provision is immeasurable. Nothing of his ever runs out. His grace and forgiveness will never end; his love and mercy are infinite. His kingdom will always be our estate. His mansion is our shelter; we will never be homeless. His food and drink will always satisfy; no one goes hungry or thirsty in heaven—ever. Heaven will be rich with joy and laughter. No one will cry or get angry; all will be at peace. There will be no more division and no more strife—no more depression, no more oppression, no more negative attitudes, and no more bad blood. The air will be 100 percent positive and pure. We can all look forward to that day. We can anticipate renewed life in heaven.

Amid global distress, God's truths remind us that the world and its troubles are only temporary. In marital distress, God's truths help us see that most of what we think is a big deal actually may not be. I've noticed, for example, a lot of what I freak out about is frivolous when I consider all that God has done for me. In the past, Brittany and I have argued over some pretty dumb stuff, from excess clutter around the house to overfilled junk drawers. Our fights have been pretty ridiculous. From piling laundry to expensive hair appointments, we have let the littlest things irritate us. We once fought over how to load the dishwasher. I once screamed at her for paying off a credit card with our savings account. My insecurity sometimes causes me to be a control freak. When I don't tell myself God's truths, I lie to myself. I say, "I am in charge of all things." When I'm not led by the Holy Spirit in my marriage, my old self resurfaces, and the past comes back to haunt me. My pride takes over, and then all that matters to me is being right. I suddenly want to win every argument and get my way.

Has your ego ever gotten the best of you? Have you ever argued with your spouse over dumb stuff? It's kind of silly when you think about it because when we get to heaven, God won't care how many husbands were right and their wives were wrong. He won't care how many arguments wives won and husbands lost. He's not interested in the battle of the sexes. All he'll be concerned with is this: "What did you do with my Son's name?" On that day, all that will matter is what you did in the name of Jesus. Viewing life in light of that day when you arrive in the kingdom reminds you that your final destination is in God's hands. Reflecting on your eternal position in Christ enables you to trust God more fully. So, while you're here on earth, lean on him completely, and give him your all, knowing he's given you *his* all. While waiting for your day in paradise, you can rely on God's Word as your source of truth, strength, and even marital peace. The Apostle Peter put it this way:

*[God's] divine power has given us everything we
need for a godly life through our knowledge of
him who called us by his own glory and goodness.
Through these he has given us his very great and
precious promises, so that through them you may
participate in the divine nature, having escaped
the corruption in the world caused by evil desires.
For this very reason, make every effort to add to
your faith goodness; and to goodness, knowledge;
and to knowledge, self-control; and to self-control,
perseverance; and to perseverance, godliness; and to
godliness, mutual affection; and to mutual affection,
love. For if you possess these qualities in increasing
measure, they will keep you from being ineffective
and unproductive in your knowledge of our LORD
Jesus Christ. But whoever does not have them is
nearsighted and blind, forgetting that they have been
cleansed from their past sins. Therefore, my brothers
and sisters, make every effort to confirm your calling
and election. For if you do these things, you will
never stumble, and you will receive a rich welcome
into the eternal kingdom of our LORD and Savior
Jesus Christ.*

—2 Pet. 1:3–11 (NIV)

God wants you to be effective and productive in your marriage. And he wants you to rest assured knowing he has worked
everything out in your favor. He doesn't want you to stumble or
fail. He wants you to stand tall (with humility, of course) and
walk with confidence, knowing that one day you will receive a
rich welcome into the eternal kingdom of our Lord and Savior
Jesus Christ, a kingdom free from marital stress and emotional

burnout, a kingdom without spousal grousing and without fuss. There will be no more worrying about finances, no more struggling for security, no more sweating to pay the bills, and no more anxiety to make ends meet. You will be wealthy in God and secure in Christ.

Speaking of finances (switching gears here), do you know what the number one reason is for divorce in our country? If you guessed money, you guessed what I would have guessed. I believe money is the top contributor to couples calling it quits. It's the most common cause of marriages ending. But different studies will show different things. I read one survey on divorce that listed lack of compatibility as the main reason. Another one stated a lack of commitment. What's interesting is that almost always when married couples go their separate ways, their focus turns to who gets what. The contention is usually over who keeps the house, the cars, the savings account, and other assets. If there are kids involved, custody is decided along with who pays child support. I have yet to come across a divorce decree that states anything other than who gets the kids and who gets the cash. There is nothing in my divorce decree from my first marriage, for example, that says I am now legally obligated to be more compatible. There's nothing about being a more committed person to my ex-wife. All it basically says is that the marriage is over and you must divvy up your stuff and write a check every month. That sounds cold and cruel, but divorce often is. Here's my point: money plays a significant part in the success, failure, and aftermath of marriages.

Work toward Your Future

My ex-wife will tell you that she was not happy. When we were married, we were dirt poor. We had to scrounge to get by. We lived in a tiny apartment on a minuscule military salary. My then-wife wasn't materialistic or anything, but I think it bothered her that I didn't provide for her and our kids. In those days, I was lazy. I had no interest in working hard for a promotion, and I was too juvenile to earn a degree. I didn't aspire to do anything grand with my life. Back then, I didn't set financial goals or have a budget. I was fine living paycheck to paycheck and really didn't care when our bank account was overdrawn. In hindsight, I wasn't being a good steward of my time or money. I was a deadbeat husband and a deadbeat dad. I didn't possess the qualities mentioned by Peter in the passage you just read. On the contrary, I was ineffective, unproductive, nearsighted, and blind, stumbling in all areas of life.

I didn't know this at the time because I wasn't a Christian, but Scripture speaks against being a deadbeat. In Paul's first letter to Timothy, we find this warning:

> *[I]f anyone does not provide for his own family, especially for members of his household, he has denied the faith and is worse than an unbeliever.*
>
> —1 Tim. 5:8 (CSB)

To be fair, this verse was written in the context of caring for widows. But if neglecting the widows in your own family makes you worse than an unbeliever, how much worse is the husband who won't provide for his own wife and kids? This verse reminds all Christian men that providing for their families is a sign of genuine faith. It is a godly notion. Paul tells them that providing for their loved ones must be a high priority. That makes sense because, throughout Scripture, we see that the provision for loved ones is a high priority to God. He set an example for us when he provided the Garden of Eden for Adam and Eve.

[T]he LORD *God planted a garden in Eden . . . and there he put the man whom he had formed. And out of the ground the* LORD *God made to spring up every tree that is pleasant to the sight and good for food.*

—Gen. 2:8–9

Since the beginning of time, God has provided for the members of his household. God provided for Adam and Eve and then Noah and his family. He provided for Abraham and Sara and then Isaac and Rebekah. God was there for Jacob at Bethel and for Joseph in Egypt. He took care of Moses in the wilderness. Then God rained down bread from heaven for the congregation of Israel. He made sure Elijah had food and water in dry land during a drought. He gave Job twice the wealth at the end of his trial, and he led Ruth to Boaz amidst her misfortune. He brought David to power and glory as king and rose Esther up to be a magnificent queen. God provided his people with warriors such as Joshua and Samson. He provided prophets such as Isaiah and Jeremiah. But most of all, he provided a Savior. God provided Jesus, born by the power of the Holy Spirit through a miraculous conception. He provided Jesus to come into the world and bring us redemption.

Jesus is also a provider. During his earthly ministry, he once fed 5,000 of his followers with a few loaves of bread and a couple of fish. Later, he did it for a group of 4,000 followers with about the same amount of food. He also miraculously provided wine out of water for guests at a wedding and fish out of an empty sea for his fisherman disciples. He provided sight to the blind, health to the sick, and strength to the weak. He even brought people back to life who had suddenly passed away. Of course, the ultimate provision was his death on the cross and shedding his blood to cleanse us from all sin (1 John 1:7–10). God infinitely provided this for us when he sent Jesus to sacrifice his life for us. Through Jesus's death and resurrection, we have faith and salvation. We who believe are forgiven, and we get to spend eternity in heaven with our Provider. This truth contains infinite value. It is worth more than anything you could imagine. It's why Jesus says to live life according to your final destination instead of your temporary place here. During his famous Sermon on the Mount, Jesus spoke these words:

> *Do not lay up for yourselves treasures on earth . . .*
> *but lay up for yourselves treasures in heaven. . . . For*
> *where your treasure is, there your heart will be also.*
> —Matt. 6:19–21

It has been said that Jesus mentioned money more than anything else throughout his ministry. If that's true, then he did it on purpose. I believe the reason was the negative effect riches can have on a person's faith. Knowing Jesus, he was probably concerned about the detriment that money can infringe upon the soul. He knew that excess money in the hands of men and women who are not focused on the kingdom will sway them from financial provision to financial ruin. Here are a couple more things Jesus said.

> *Watch out! Be on your guard against all kinds of greed;*
> *life does not consist in an abundance of possessions.*
> —Luke 12:15 (NIV)

> *Sell your possessions, and give to the needy. Provide*
> *yourselves with moneybags that do not grow old, with*
> *a treasure in the heavens that does not fail.*
> —Luke 12:33

If God allows us to store up treasures in heaven, then how we steward our money matters. It means we can't be deadbeats. But it also means we can't be greedy. We should be considerate to choose others over our own comfort. We should consider choosing the members of our own household over materialism and greed. In fact, I believe there is an immediate call to a kingdom-work-effort in every Christian home the moment a man leaves his father and mother to hold fast to his wife. A united front should commence when the two become one flesh, one that consists of hard-working, generous spouses. All decisions involving money should reflect God's call on their lives, not a desire to be filthy rich. All purchases, possessions, savings, and investments should be decided on together as husband and wife as often as possible. That way, each husband and wife will be considerate of their spouse's reward in heaven.

Guard Your Future Together

When Brittany and I got married, we started a checking account in both our names. We also opened a joint savings account. The finances were no longer "my money" and "her money" but "our money." Today, all our credit cards and loans are together, and we file our taxes together. All her debt is my debt, and vice versa. All my financial setbacks are hers, and in every financial crisis, we stick it out together. When we give financially, we give on behalf of both of us. Together we decide the amounts of our tithes and offerings. As one flesh, we choose what ministries we support and what causes we donate to. This is our way of providing ourselves with a treasure in heaven that does not fail. It's not a perfect plan by any stretch. Sometimes we overspend. Sometimes we make mistakes. On occasion, we debate about what we should and shouldn't purchase. We have disagreements on how to save and invest our money. But the important thing is that we never lose sight of the fact that we're in it together. We see our finances as a gift from God and therefore make every effort to be good stewards of every penny.

We know that temptation is always lying in wait. It never goes away. It is a lifelong constant. It entices us with things we don't need such as the latest model luxury vehicle or a bigger flat-screen TV. Temptation doesn't want us to save money to drown in debt. It wants us to keep up with the Joneses and buy a bigger house we can't afford. It wants us to be glamorous, lured by the most expensive amenities and accessories. Temptation tells us we deserve a more lavish lifestyle. Sure, it might be fine to have nice stuff but not if it causes us to go against God's Word. If our marriage becomes a fashion show for all to envy, then we've missed the point of what God has called us to do with our money. Here's a passage that comes to mind when considering this.

> *As for the rich in this present age, charge them not to be haughty, nor to set their hopes on the uncertainty of riches, but on God, who richly provides us with everything to enjoy. They are to do good, to be rich in good works, to be generous and ready to share, thus storing up treasure for themselves as a good foundation for the future, so that they may take hold of that which is truly life.*
>
> —1 Tim. 6:17–19

Paul doesn't beat around the bush here. He says to avoid anything that would deter us from being rich in good works. This Scripture is clear. Never let money distract you from living on mission. Mishandling money weakens your kingdom-work-effort and makes you ungenerous and unprepared to share. I would hate to put my marriage in a situation that would rob me and my wife of a good foundation for the future. I would never want to prevent us from taking hold of what is truly life. I trust you feel the same way about your marriage.

Do you know what's crazy? Even after hearing what the Bible says about handling finances, money remains a huge deal to us. We're still tempted to go hard after that cold hard cash. We'll still consider earning the wealthiest lifestyle one could possibly attain. And a lot of husbands (myself included) will be tempted to stop at nothing to get there. We'll work 80 hours a week and travel to wherever the money is. We'll work nonstop because the truth is that we love money. We are obsessed with it. We can't get away from it because we need it. Money provides a sense of security and certainty, even though it is a false sense. And the more money we get, the more secure we feel. The more purchases we're able to make, the more confident we are of being in control.

We end up wanting more and more money. Some of us are overcome by greed, and others become scrimpy and cheap. Some of us hide our money in a safe so no one can touch it. Others lock it in a vault so no one can access it. It gets tucked away in a deposit box at a bank guarded by security. We'll tell ourselves things like "This is my money; I earned it" or "This is mine; I worked hard for it." That may be true, but if your money turns you into a rich snob instead of a sacrificial giver, something's wrong. If your wealth makes you haughty and not ready to share, then you've missed the point of the Lord's provision. A common theme throughout the entire Bible is that everything we have is what we receive from God. Every good gift comes from our Provider. Everything we own and acquire is because the good Lord made it so. We came into this world with nothing, and we will leave this world with nothing.

If we're being honest, our lives are easier when we have money. The more we have, the safer we feel. The more we lay up for ourselves treasures on earth, the better off we think we'll be. There is some truth to that logic, but there's a huge danger to it as well. Otherwise, Jesus wouldn't have cautioned us about it. Here's his warning:

No one can serve two masters, for either he will hate the one and love the other, or he will be devoted to the one and despise the other. You cannot serve God and money.

—Matt. 6:24

That doesn't mean it's a sin to have excess money. It's not evil to enjoy your money, and it's not a sin for couples to be rich. There were plenty of wealthy men and women in the history of God's people. And today there are plenty of devout husbands and wives in the Body of Christ who have been blessed financially. You can be a Christian and be a millionaire. You can be a godly individual and be a billionaire. After all, the more a servant receives, the more able they are to give, as long as they give cheerfully.

Invest in Your Future Together

Some of you reading this are ahead of the game. You are extremely generous. You love to give, and you love sharing your wealth in the name of Jesus. Some of you already know there is wisdom in being smart with money. You're already planning for retirement, kids' educations, rainy days, and things like that. But this is an area I think all husbands and wives can continuously grow in. And if there is a right way for us to manage our money, then there is most certainly a wrong way. If there is a godly way to handle our finances, then there most certainly is an ungodly way. The right way is the way that brings glory to God, peace to marriages, and unity to families. Couples should give and receive in a way that brings praise to God and demonstrates love to people. The better we steward our money by investing in the kingdom, the more we lay up for ourselves treasures in heaven.

These instructions that Jesus gives, along with the pastoral wisdom that Paul offers, apply to us and our spouses. Since we are provided so much in Christ, we shouldn't let something like deadbeat-ism or greed ruin our marriages. Rather, we should utilize our finances to help sustain our marital commitments. We should use our financial blessings to assist us in cultivating things such as love, unity, and peace. I'm not saying we should buy our way into our spouse's heart. What I am saying is that God gives us resources for the marital support we'll need. If we turn around and use it for greed, we'll most likely end up in despair. If the resources God provides aren't used with initiative, they could turn us into good-for-nothing couch potatoes.

God knows lifelong love isn't easy in our generation. I'll be the first to admit that staying married is hard work. God knows I want to be faithful to my wife. He knows I want the opportunity to provide food and shelter for my family. He knows I want to afford date nights and vacations. These are things that help strengthen marital bonds. But God's plan rarely remains within my comfort zone. My wife and I went through tough financial seasons for God to save our marriage. We had some marital growing pains along the way. We needed to invest in a marriage counselor to help us. We had to be shown that marriage is never 50-50. Marriage requires 100 percent from both spouses. The point is that all husbands and wives need to be willing to make sacrifices. We should be ready to give up anything and be willing to lay down our lives as Jesus did.

God wants us to give the way that he gives, sacrifice how Jesus sacrificed, and help others like the Holy Spirit helps others. How do we do that? Well, we have to be all in. I love that phrase—all in. I heard it for the first time while watching a movie about gambling. There is a scene where the main character pushes all his poker chips into the middle of the table. He bets all his winnings on the belief that he is holding the highest hand. He risks everything he has to come out on top. But he doesn't do so blindly. He makes his decision based on every carefully played hand, consistently calculating the odds and adhering to the rules of the game. He goes all in with complete confidence. There is a somewhat similar scene in the Bible that demonstrates the way we should go all in. I say somewhat similar because there is no gambling involved. Instead, it's an act of faith. It's not a game that's being played; it's real life. And the person setting the example is not a man but a woman. It goes like this:

> *Jesus sat down opposite the place where the offerings were put and watched the crowd putting their money into the temple treasury. Many rich people threw in large amounts. But a poor widow came and put in two very small copper coins, worth only a few cents. Calling his disciples to him, Jesus said, "Truly I tell you, this poor widow has put more into the treasury than all the others. They all gave out of their wealth; but she, out of her poverty, put in everything—all she had to live on."*
> —Mark 12:41–44 (NIV)

So much is revealed in this passage of Scripture. For starters, these verses prove that Jesus isn't interested in our stuff. Again, he doesn't want our prized possessions; he wants our hearts. What was dear to Jesus in this scene was not the rich people's leftovers but the poor widow's first fruits. What was valuable to him was not the wealthy's big bucks but the poor widow's chump change. She was going all in while the rich were playing a safe bet. The wealthy were taking care of themselves first before giving to God. The poor widow gave first to God, knowing he would take care of her. This offering showed her devotion to the Lord and her utter dependence on him. She was serving God, not money, so she chose to fully commit to the one who provides. She would have no part in serving two masters.

I like to think the Holy Spirit spoke to her beforehand, perhaps through something Jesus said in past teachings. Or maybe it was just the Lord's work in her heart. Whatever her reason, Jesus brought special attention to her act of sacrificial giving. He told his disciples that her kingdom-work effort held more value than the rich because of how she gave, not what she gave. By pointing this out, he reminded his disciples that blessed are the poor and hungry for they will one day be satisfied in heaven. He also showed them a living testimony of a true disciple, an example of a follower of Christ he had previously described to them.

> *Whoever wants to be my disciple must deny themselves*
> *and take up their cross daily and follow me.*
> —Luke 9:23 (NIV)

Go All In Together

The people of God must be all in because of the evil desire that threatens humanity. Christians must be all in to combat the chaos and adversity that plagues our planet. And since our marriages reflect the image of God and the Bride of Christ, husbands and wives should be all in to heal not harm, to fix not break. They must be all in for good, not bad, to love and not hate. You and your spouse must be all in to give sacrificially to God and to each other.

When following Jesus, there is no room to be selfish. For every husband who spends too much time on the golf course, there is a wife who spends too much time feeling lonely and left out. For every husband who is endlessly playing video games and binge-watching TV shows, there is a wife who endlessly feels neglected and rejected. For every husband who works nonstop, there is a wife who needs more love nonstop. I'm not picking on the men. Wives are equally responsible for cultivating companionship and promoting togetherness. That doesn't mean spouses can't have alone time or do things on their own, but it should never be at the expense of your marital unity. God desires oneness between husbands and wives who deeply love each other. They should be experiencing closeness, not distance.

Accepting someone as your lawfully wedded spouse before God shouldn't be a half-hearted deal. Imagine being in the middle of your wedding ceremony with the person you are about to marry and instead of saying "I do" you say "I guess." Guys, imagine getting down on one knee, asking the woman of your dreams to marry you, and she says, "We can try it out and see if it works." Ladies, imagine you've just been proposed to. Pretend you've just said yes to the big question, and right after getting engaged, your new fiancé says, "Hey, if it doesn't work, we can just get divorced." Before anyone is pronounced husband and wife, they should be willing to put in everything. They should be willing to give all they have. When you stand at the altar and say "I do," essentially what you're saying is "I'm all in."

If there's one thing I want you to learn from this book, it's this: Treat your marriage like it's the best hand you could ever be dealt—a royal flush. The odds are in your favor for success, so go all in. Jesus went all in for his Bride. Now you can go all in for your spouse.

> *And whatever you do, whether in word or deed, do it all in the name of the Lord Jesus, giving thanks to God the Father through him.*
>
> —Col. 3:17 (NIV)

One Last Thing

This is straight from the heart, so please read considering everything I have written so far. I've most likely said something in one or more of these chapters that you either disagree with, are wrestling with, or were maybe offended by. That's a good sign. Here's why: We can't read books and think that everything the author says is exactly what we want to hear. No good book should ever be like that. The Bible isn't even like that. In fact, the message of the cross is one of the most offensive things we will ever hear. The gospel calls us out as sinners. It says we are hopeless. It says we are lost and that we can do nothing for ourselves.

The gospel explains how broken we are. It brings to light everything you and I are doing wrong. Then it tells us there is only one person in human history who did it right. As you process what you've read, keep that in mind. My goal is not to bash anyone or discourage anyone. I set out to do quite the opposite. I care about you, and I care about your marriage. If I haven't written anything that seems controversial to you, praise God. But keep reading because I have a few more things to say.

Too many of us are living with one foot out the door. It used to be that couples got divorced because they weren't happy. Nowadays, spouses leave not because they're unhappy but because they think they can be happier with someone else. Those someone elses' are usually richer or better looking. They typically have higher-paying jobs and bigger houses. They can possibly provide better sex or more financial security. Quite often those someone elses aren't jerks or nags. They don't have tempers; they're not abrasive. They're nicer and less confrontational than your spouse. They make you feel alive, important, and giddy. There's only one thing wrong with that. None of those are grounds for divorce—ever. There is only one reason anyone should get divorced. This is Jesus talking:

> *And I say to you: whoever divorces his wife, except for sexual immorality, and marries another, commits adultery.*
>
> —Matt. 9:19

That's what Jesus said. He was responding to someone who asked if it was lawful to divorce for any reason. Jesus makes it clear that unless a spouse cheats or the marriage is violated in a sexually immoral way, they should not end their marriage. If you're in a tough situation and you're wondering, "What would Jesus do?" that's the counsel he gives.

That doesn't mean if you are suffering from spousal abuse you should remain in the home. There are ways to get help, and there are ways to get out without getting divorced. That also doesn't mean you must stay if there is a danger to you and your children. Again, there are ways to keep you and your children safe from harm without getting divorced. The important thing to remember is that God is always working. Everything happens for a reason, and whatever happens is all part of God's plan for your life, which, by the way, works out for good. Never forget this verse:

> *And we know that for those who love God all things work together for good, for those who are called to his purpose.*
>
> —Rom. 8:28

What this means is that amid whatever current suffering you might be experiencing, you must never forget that in Christ you are headed for future happiness. Whatever pain you undergo, God eventually overcomes it with unending joy and relief. When my first marriage ended, my ex-wife had grounds for divorce. I wasn't a Christian yet, but because I ended up with Brittany, everything worked out for good. Know that divorce is always wrong. Divorce is always bad. But thank God there is grace available for it. Thank Jesus for dying on the cross and forgiving people for their divorces. And thank the Holy Spirit for his power to overcome bad fruit by bringing to life good fruit. I pray that you and your spouse will be a strong united tree planted firmly in the love of God, which never fails.

Marriage is one day at a time. It's one hour at a time. Make every moment count by committing yourself to the daily and hourly success of your marriage. It will be one of the hardest things you'll ever do, but trust me, it will be one of the most memorable things you'll ever do. You will need help, so please go out and get it. Don't be ashamed of whatever your situation is because you're not alone. Remember that God is always watching over us, waiting for the day to bring us all home forever. Below is one more Bible passage I want you to know. Commit to memorizing it. Learn it. Love it. Live it.

> *All of you, clothe yourselves with humility toward one another, because, "God opposes the proud but shows favor to the humble." Humble yourselves, therefore, under God's mighty hand, that he may lift you up in due time. Cast all your anxiety on him because he cares for you. Be alert and of sober mind. Your enemy the devil prowls around like a roaring lion looking for someone to devour. Resist him, standing firm in the*

faith, because you know that the family of believers throughout the world is undergoing the same kind of sufferings. And the God of all grace, who called you to his eternal glory in Christ, after you suffered a little while, will himself restore you and make you strong, firm and steadfast. To him be the power for ever and ever. Amen.

—1 Pet. 5:5–11 (NIV)

Acknowledgments

Many people contributed to the writing of this book and helped me along this journey. My wife, Brittany, has taught me much about being a good husband, lover, and friend. I am grateful for her. To my parents, Everett and Estella Tellez, who care for me in so many ways. To my in-laws, Steve and Terri Trickel: Your love inspires me. I hope to be as generous and as kind as you. To my kids: Michael, Nicholas, Dakota, Trace, Ezra, and Jack. Your smiles keep me going. To my pastors: Dr. Bruce Webb, Matt Poe, and Tierce Green. I will never forget your wisdom and support. To our marriage counselor: Hans Molegraaf. You saved my marriage, Brother. Without your ministry and your prayers, Brittany and I would have drifted apart.

There is also a list of great leaders, teachers, pastors, and authors, whom I have never met, but who taught me a great deal of things for this book. Dr. R.C. Sproul, founder of Ligonier Ministries. John Piper, founder of Desiring God ministries. Sinclair Ferguson, Chancellor's Professor of Systematic Theology at Reformed Theological Seminary. Derek Thomas, Professor of Theology and Pastor. Warren Wiersbe, Pastor, and Writer. Gary Thomas, Christian author, and pastor. Although I don't know any of these men personally, their expertise on marriage has been invaluable to me.

Of course, none of this would be possible without God, our Father, to whom we owe our entire lives. To him be honor and glory forever and ever. Amen.

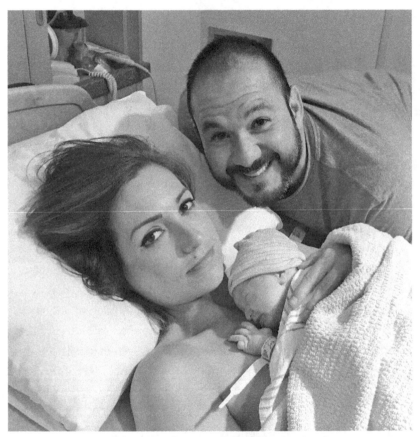

Genesis 1:28, "Be fruitful and multiply…"